"Connie Soth has written an excellent introduction to the spiritual life from a unique point of view – one suffering from insomnia. Many people find that the most creative time for prayer and relationship with God is in the middle of the night. They seem to be awakened by the Spirit and given time without any interruptions. The author of *Insomnia: God's Night School* has shown how this waking time can be one of great spiritual creativity. She knows the depth of the spiritual life and gives specific methods of using this God-given time. Her emphasis is on God and allowing the Spirit to lead us through these nightly sessions to full life in this world and into the utter fulfillment that lies within the mysterious vista of eternity.

"I am delighted that the author has written a whole book on this practice of listening to God in the depth of the night–a practice that along with listening to dreams opened the reality of God and the spiritual life to me."

Professor Morton Kelsey, Professor of Theology at Notre Dame University, Author of The Other Side of Silence

Insomnia

God's
Night School

Connie Soth

Power
Books

Fleming H. Revell Company
Old Tappan, New Jersey

Library of Congress Cataloging-in-Publication Data

Soth, Connie.
    Insomnia: God's night school.

    1. Insomniacs—Prayer books and devotions—English.
I. Title
BV4910.4.S65   1989   248.8'6   88-32487
ISBN 0-8007-5305-4

Copyright © 1989 by Connie Soth
Published by the Fleming H. Revell Company
Old Tappan, New Jersey 07675
Printed in the United States of America

Over a period of seven years, when my book was struggling to be, Madeleine L'Engle wrote faithfully to me with words of encouragement. Her generous spirit best represents the vital camaraderie other writer friends also displayed. They, and she, willingly took time from their own creative efforts, assignments, commitments, and deadlines to encourage and affirm me.

To you, Madeleine,
and to that coterie of supportive writers who
echoed your conviction, "the world needs your book,"
thank you

Contents ★ _____

★ ──────────────────────────────────

Invitation to the Reader

What do you do when you can't sleep?

Most people say they will do anything, try anything, and ever-growing stacks of books offer a myriad of clever how-to's, all the way from hypnosis to freaky diets to occultish practices to help them.

Doctors, on hearing the cry "I can't sleep!" promptly write prescriptions for sleeping pills.

So—everybody agrees that not sleeping is bad for you, maybe even hazardous to your health—right?

Wrong.

Not being able to get to sleep at night or waking up in the middle of the night can be the best thing that ever happened to you—if you read the signals correctly.

Having your sleep disturbed may be God's only way of getting your attention because He can't squeeze into your busy daytime schedule.

Why bring God into it? Well, first, He has said He cares about every detail of our lives. Second, it's not so much "bringing God into it" as admitting He is already there.

If you and I were having coffee together today and you were seeking sympathy because you have bouts of insomnia, I would say, "Look, so what if you aren't sleeping. Here's your chance to ask God what insomnia is good for."

Insomnia: God's Night School is my way of "having coffee" with all readers. Together, we can explore the reasons for insomnia and find some answers.

My part will be to share how God answered this question for me by showing me how to cross the invisible threshold from fear of insomnia to mastery of it.

Before I begin, read through the questionnaire preceding chapter 1 and, for your own information, record your responses on a separate piece of paper. You may learn about some aspects of sleeplessness you have avoided thinking about—or didn't know about. Often, just considering an old problem from a different angle will reveal the solution.

By the time you finish this book, I hope you will be convinced that *all* insomnia, whatever its cause, can be helped through the God-encounter from which unique peace flows, a healing balm for all hurts and fears. The insomniac who thanks God for wakeful times in the night, believing that He will bring something good out of it, has already begun to receive the blessing of peace.

So if you've wondered what use it is to be alive when all you do is struggle from one sleepless night to the next, take a look at my experience as a possible road map for your own life journey. If you are willing to listen, you are already on the right road.

Questionnaire

1. How long have you had insomnia? In what ways has it affected your life?

2. Is your family sympathetic? Indifferent? Hostile? Other?

3. What causes your insomnia?

4. What do you do about your inability to sleep? Has any one remedy helped much?

5. What is the pattern of your insomnia? (Examples: Can't get to sleep; wake up in the middle of the night; wake up too early in the morning.)

6. What fears seem connected with your insomnia?

7. Is sleep necessary for maintaining good health? Do you think lack of sleep can be life-threatening? Please expand answers.

8. What is the difference between *sleeplessness* and *wakefulness*?

9. In your opinion, are *rest* and *sleep* synonymous? If not, why not?

10. Mention any books or articles on sleep disorder research you have read. Were any helpful? Specify.

11. Have you tried relaxation therapy, sleep therapy, or transcendental meditation? If any helped, please describe how.

12. Have you ever visited a sleep laboratory? Were you a client? If so, relate your experience and results.

13. Might your insomnia have an emotional base? Are you worried about members of your family? What about a spiritual dimension? Note your conclusions for future use.

14. If you have already tried a spiritual solution (prayer, Bible reading, meditation), what was your approach? Did it help?

15. If you read when you can't sleep, what do you read? Does it help?

16. If you read the Bible, what kind of help do you expect?

17. If you received help by reading the Bible, please cite passages, chapter and verse.

18. Do you think God cares whether or not you can sleep? Explain.

19. When others can sleep and you can't, how do you feel?

20. Please turn to the end of this book and read the "Nine Beatitudes for Those Who Lie Awake." Put your reactions on paper to look at again after you finish the book. Then reread these "beatitudes."

21. If you would like to share your answers to this questionnaire or tell me about your insomnia, or anything having to do with your insomnia experience, write to me in care of the publisher. I will answer every letter I receive.

Insomnia
God's
Night School

One ★ _____

Learning to
Listen in
the Silent Night

Running, running down an endless dark hall, fear pounding in my chest, I struggle to breathe at the same time I jerk futilely at the back door, unable to unlock it in my panic.

At last I stumble outside on to the porch, trembling and gasping for air.

Was it a nightmare? No, I was awake during this new link in a long chain of nights when sleep betrayed me. On nights when I couldn't sleep, my bed turned into a torture rack. Feverish "what ifs" and "why didn't I's" crowded in beside me, uninvited bed partners. If I did drift off, sunken in fatigue, sleep would too often end in this race down the hall. Pitiless claustrophobia, crouching ever ready in the shadows, sprang the moment I relaxed.

Once outside you'd think my fears would evaporate, soothed by the normalcy of fresh air and quiet dark, but even the night sky seemed an enemy, pressing malevolently down to smother me.

Finally, after many dreary nights of rushing outside shaking and gasping, sure I was forever doomed to play this deadly night game, out of nowhere a steady, cool voice came. The message was to calm myself; to realize I wouldn't die of panic; to face my problems.

To face my problems. It was true—my rush down the hall was merely acting out my fruitless efforts to escape. The rapidly widening rift between my husband and me over child-raising methods, disagreements about almost every facet of married life, his incomprehension of my newfound spiritual interest, had so exhausted me that daily I retreated into daytime naps—two, three hours of oblivion as addictive and useless as an alcoholic stupor—to avoid thinking. Although I knew sleeping during the day would bring sleepless nights, I no longer cared. And now, just when my stress level had reached boil-over stage, claustrophobia was again invading my life.

Again was the key word. I thought I'd conquered my fear of being trapped, first experienced when our three sons were much younger and I feared I was an inadequate mother. The doctor had assured me then that my pounding heart and smothery feeling came not from heart trouble, as I feared, but from trying too hard.

"Don't worry so much. Just enjoy them while they're young," he advised cheerily. "All too soon they will be grown up and gone."

At his brisk words of counsel, the claustrophobia monster curled up and died. But now, ten years later, here it was again, worse than ever and complicated by insomnia.

"But I'm not alone this time—am I, Lord?"

No, here was the wonderful difference. Release of His Spirit through a new encounter with Christ had generated fresh spiritual energy. With Him I could do anything, defeating the night terrors included. God waited to show me a new thing.

Now, the morning devotions I'd doggedly performed, even though sleepless nights weighted my eyelids as I tried to study, began to bring my problems into focus. That same cool, steady voice in my ears showed me startling truths for my life, as startling as when I was sixteen and had put on my first pair of badly needed glasses.

For as long as I could remember, trees had been merely a green blur, but with glasses on I could see bouquets of artfully designed, exquisitely shaped, individual leaves, each one a masterpiece of craftsmanship.

In this same way I began to see reassurances about rest and sleep everywhere I read in the Bible. I could hardly write them down fast enough.

Then, the Spirit blew from an unexpected quarter. . . .

One night when I went to bed, laboring to control my fear of insomnia and claustrophobia, I observed that being awake and alone with the silence wasn't so bad. Slipping out of bed quietly, so as not to disturb my husband, I walked softly through the dark house and sat down on the sofa to think things over.

No one was demanding that I do this or that; the telephone was silent; I was excused from the mundane work of housewifery. As I listened, I realized how scarce a commodity silence is in our society, except for the sheepherder in the Montana wilds or the lone backpacker trudging the Cascade trails. I thought about the seething caldron of noise most of us not only endure but add to by talking incessantly or by turning on radio, stereo, or TV.

Actually, I'd always enjoyed little stretches of quiet, I mused. During those years when our sons were growing up, noise was the climate of our home. If my husband wasn't hurrying off to work at the office, he was hurrying home to complete various house-finishing projects, adding the scream of saw or the pounding of hammer to the general cacophony. Our boys insisted they couldn't study without a radio blaring at one elbow but gave in to my desperate cry that they turn it down.

Now, sitting in this unaccustomed silence, for the first time in my life I wondered if we hadn't succumbed to a society that teaches us to say "he turns me off" and "that turns me on" as though we were merely machines manipulated by a switch. This led to the uncomfortable thought, *Do we flick God on and off, too?* But I wasn't ready to think about that—yet.

I hadn't decided whether this silence was a threat or a promise, but as I listened to the ordinary night sounds I told myself I didn't have to be afraid of distant traffic, that dog barking the next street over, the furnace clicking on and off, certainly not the funny, sleepy chirp outside my window. These random, comfortable noises, furniture of the night, I could safely circumnavigate.

Total silence—now, that's a different matter. Maybe that's why, I pondered, I like the drumming of rain on the roof, the gurgle of water in the gutters; why I feel lulled by the rush of wind in the trees in our back field. But on nights when all I can hear is the ringing of silence, when the strange *thub-dup* of my heartbeat pounds in my ears, when I can imagine the blood pulsing through my veins, a disturbing sense of my own mortality looms.

As I reflected, other thoughts edged in, carrying unwanted baggage of regrets and remorse, resentments and rejections—all those *re* prefixed words yearning for another chance. I remembered naturalist/poet Loren Eiseley's insights: "Our minds are haunted by night terrors that arise from the subterranean domain of racial and private memories."

Was I using rain or wind—or for that matter, the mundane hum of an air conditioner—to blot out thoughts suspended just beneath the surface of knowing, thoughts that might leap out and fill my night unbearably with "mind chatter" such as I'd just experienced? In later years I would read H. Wayne Pipkin's advice about clearing your mind of this static when preparing to meditate, and I would get a flash of recognition.[1] At the time of my insomnia, however, I was only beginning to understand. How, I wondered, could I clear my mental decks of this subliminal muttering?

As though He'd been waiting for my question, the quiet Presence behind the silence again made Himself known to me.

"Why don't you ask Me?"

"Father? God? Is that You? Oh—were you waiting for a time when You could get my attention?"

"What do *you* think?"

"Well, I do tend to put You on hold. . . ."

Just the touch of whimsy I needed. Even as these thoughts distracted me from my fear of not sleeping, my breathing calmed, my heart slowed from a gallop to a steadier beat, and a door inside my huddled spirit swung open to let the fresh air of the Holy Spirit move freely through.

The smog of claustrophobia/insomnia blowing away like smoke on the wind, I began at long last to look squarely at my claim that I live by Romans 12:2, "Don't let the world around you squeeze you into its own mould . . ." (PHILLIPS) and to admit that I had indeed allowed the world, like an iron maiden of the spirit, to close around me. I was impaled on the spikes of conformity.

Pictures crowded my mind. In one I saw myself swept up by the tumult of daily events, running right past where Jesus sat waiting for me beside the hot, dusty road I'd chosen. What a luxury to stop dead in my tracks, deliberately turn back, and drop at His feet. Now the same cool, revitalizing Water of Life He gave the Samaritan woman flowed from Him to me and my tense body relaxed. How odd of God, I reflected, not to give me a quick fix of sleep but instead to use the sleeplessness I dreaded to draw me closer to Himself.

What are You up to, Lord?

Since then, I've read of sleep therapists who warn against what they term *secondary satisfactions*, cautioning against giving yourself a consolation prize for not being able to get to sleep or for waking up in the middle of the night. Eating a chocolate eclair every night at two o'clock or eagerly sipping the warm milk of sympathy from insomnia-free friends—it makes no difference; both perpetuate the problem. So was I doing something similar, looking forward to God's company in the night? No, unlike food or sympathy, God was good for me.

Once I'd accepted the silence and being awake, listening in the night also taught me to thank God in advance for whatever He would reveal in His Book, and to begin a midnight journal to preserve the insights He'd already given me. I sensed God there with me as I studied and wrote. Not that He offered Himself as a sort of cosmic teddy bear, a snuggly bulwark against night terrors. He did, however, protect me from despair as my shortcomings became apparent, as He forced me to look at how solipsistic I'd become.

My thoughts, *my* needs, *my* feelings had crowded out everything and everybody else to become the center of my universe.

God showed me I was staggering under a load of grudges that would founder a mule. He exposed my cozy little "Me 'n' Jesus" club of which I was president and sole member. With persistent, tough love He pushed me into a corner where there was nothing to look at except the stark right angles of self-centeredness.

Agreeing with God that you are a sinner, I discovered, is difficult and frightening—but only until you actually do it. Then He gives you the courage to admit your guilt. Doubts about His trustworthiness dissolve as you practice thinking, *What if I believed You love me without reservation?*

As possibility grew into reality, as understanding came of why I was embarrassed to say, "I'm guilty and I'm sorry," I began to see why repentance and confession seem so melodramatic. The answer? A century of subtle campaign by the devotees of Sigmund Freud has resulted in society's capitulation to one man's theory. We swallowed the camel/lie that sin doesn't exist. Also, too often going into analysis means picking the scab off the sore that poisons life but doing nothing to heal it. The scalpel Freud proposed we use to lay bare our private lives—confession— is safe only when wielded by God and cleansed with the antiseptic of forgiveness. He is the Surgeon who heals as skillfully as He cuts away the putrescence of sin.

At first, to trust God so totally was a lurching ride on a rutted road. From habit, I tried to protect myself, making excuses and justifying my actions. Regular practice of confession, though, soon began filling in the potholes.

Then one night I heard myself ask God to cleanse my unconscious as well as my conscious thoughts. I reminded myself

21

of Peter, who refused to let Jesus wash his feet until the Lord told him how vital it was. Then, impetuous as always, Peter exclaimed, "Not my feet only; wash my hands and head as well!" (John 13:6–9 NEB).

Although Peter had much to learn about servanthood, he symbolized every future believer who would offer a stained and soiled life to God, crying, "All of me, Lord—wash all of me!"

Given this insight, every confession I risked, every resolution I made to be more obedient, brought God's love closer.

Even so, James' Epistle stopped me like a washed-out road. Begun gently enough, the letter seemed written to me:

Dear Connie,
    Draw near to God and He will draw near to you.

James 4:8

What a loving invitation. But then James' tone changed. He demanded that I admit I was a sinner. I protested—I'd already done that!

Still, the words pounded away like a mallet driving home nails, telling me I must "get my soiled hands clean" and seek God's help to "purify my heart of spiritual adultery." I was *ordered* to "be deeply penitent," to "weep over my disloyalty," and to "feel dejection and heartfelt shame."

Appalled, I protested to God, "Lord, can this be You speaking through James? I thought You were supposed to be my Comforter."

Prompted to read on anyway, I heard James' voice change again. He now promised that if I would dare to be this vulnerable

I would soon feel God's strong hand bringing me back to my feet. From across the centuries, my brother James assured me, "If you humble yourself in the presence of the Lord, He will exalt you" (verse 10).

Apparently, I had mistaken a single episode of cleansing for the whole book on sanctification. Another error of our age, instant satisfaction, had tripped me up.

After this breakthrough, despite inordinate attacks of self-pity and nights when I shoved aside God's help, illogically preferring to be wretched, my fight became a birth event. God was midwifing a new person in those long, silent nights, His love never faltering in the face of my obstinacy.

Now, more often than not, I could go to sleep without difficulty. Then something new began to happen. A few hours into the night I would wake up as though to the ring of an alarm—but not the one ticking on the nightstand. This silent signal, I learned, meant that I should leave my bed and bring Bible and midnight journal to the dining room table, a staging area where God waited to give me marching orders.

One correcting word from the Lord appeared in Psalms 127:2 (AMP), to which I again felt impelled to add, "Dear Connie":

It is vain for you to rise up early, to take rest late, to eat the bread of [anxious] toil; for He gives [blessings] to His beloved in sleep.

How clearly meant for me. I had tried work and exercise, driving myself over the edge of fatigue, having discarded daytime naps as an escape. And how often I'd delayed going to bed, dreaded the wide-eyed hours. The "bread of anxious toil" had given me nothing but spiritual dyspepsia. Why not claim this promise?

So I prayed:

> Lord, I believe You when You say I am one of Your beloved. I can trust You to reveal Your reasons for allowing my insomnia. Whenever You are ready. I can wait without fear.

I think He answered by prompting me to go back to my concordance again, this time to look for references on prayer. I was beginning to wonder if my long-held grudges and impatience with other people's flaws had been directly responsible for my lack of ability to sleep. Again He spoke:

> Connie, give up your grievances. Stop counting and adding columns of wrongs done to you, gloating over them like a miser counting her gold. I want to make you more like Myself, even if it takes all night—every night.

Then, late one summer evening, I learned how powerfully He moves once you ask for His help.

As unable to sleep as though I'd never learned anything about insomnia, I sat on the back steps of our home, anger and hurt feelings simmering and seething like Mount St. Helen, ready to explode. Over and over, I recalled a harsh criticism flung at me after a class I'd taught at a conference. I couldn't leave it alone, the way your tongue goes back to explore a sore tooth.

Magnificent rebuttals I'd not made, crushing rejoinders I'd not voiced, echoed and thundered in my mind. To this inner clamor my stricken conscience added a rebuke for not being "very Christian" (forgiving) about it all.

Stifled indignation erupted before I could choke back the words. I cried out in a stage whisper:

God—how could she say such things to me? When she said I talked too much it almost killed me! She went on and on . . . I felt like such a fool. Why did You let her? I think I'm mad at You, too, God—yes, I *am* mad at You . . . so go ahead, strike me down—I don't care.

My tears and fiercely whispered words collided for some time, until with a little shock I realized that the crickets still sang their summer song; the stars sparkled no less; a passing breeze idly rummaged in the birch leaves—and no bolt of divine wrath sizzled out of the night. Since I wasn't yet a cinder, I thought I might as well get rid of all my mixed-up feelings. My dilemma of not being able to sleep forgotten, I let anger pour out.

At last, I admitted that I must face up to my own sins and leave my critic's shortcomings to God; an inner easing began. How ridiculously simple, after all, to say to God, ". . . and another thing . . ." and shed all the burdens warping my life. Drained, I finally sat limp and quiet. Then that patient, calm voice inquired, "Anything else, Connie, My daughter? Anything else you wanted to tell Me?"

In a flash of insight I knew, as though I'd always known, that others may get impatient with my many words, but God will listen as long as I have anything to tell Him. He will never interrupt or change the subject or want to talk about Himself instead, the way humans do. He will never scold me or rehash what I should have done. Only when I come to the end of my recital of woe will He gently or firmly correct according to my need. First must come the purging of hostility, anger, and fear. Could I, I wonder, have learned this at any other time but during the nights when I couldn't sleep?

I learned, too, that when you talk to God it's no use putting on your company face, praying only the prayers you think will please Him to hear. He knows all about you anyway—including everything you try to hide down some back alley of your mind.

Catharsis first, then cleansing, then the invitation to "enter His Rest"—an inner assurance irradiating your being with such wholeness and health no amount of sleep can ever give. To be at peace with God is to glimpse the perfect affinity God planned when He created humankind to be His eternal good companions. In spite of the Fall, He still offers Himself as our Best Friend.

Now that I know Him, the words of a human friend, Frank Laubach, spark to bright, new life. He says that if you have asked God to fill the little jar of your life with His spiritual power, you must next ask Him to knock out the bottom, to make you a conduit through which His healing energy can flow to others.[2] With tender understanding, I now look at the faces of others, so haggard with fatigue and fear about not sleeping, and I want to say, "Come—let Jesus show you what to do with your sleepless nights."

He wants to teach each of us to listen in the silent night and to say, "Speak, Lord, for Your servant listens," as well as, "I'm glad You are listening, Lord, because I have a lot to tell you."

Whatever else He shows you to do with your insomnia, He can teach you to be a helping hand and a compassionate heart, to be a self-forgetting intercessor who listens as intently to others as He listens to you, ready to dive into the mainstream of His purposes without asking how deep the current. When a restless night comes your way again it need not worry you; your attitude toward being awake can be forever changed because you've been to God's night school. If you need a refresher course He will call school back into session. He is willing to teach the same lessons of life as many times as you require to learn them.

I often attempt to take charge of my own life again—no doubt more than I relinquish my will to God—but even so, just knowing God will not lose patience with me endows life with a richer texture. Wayward though I am, I know I will never have to go back to fighting the Dark by myself.

Sometimes, as I think about the way God taught me to conquer my fear of insomnia, I wonder:

Lord, why do You stand by and let us sink deeper and deeper into the quicksand of our mistakes? And why do You step to our rescue only when we've sunk up to our eyes in trouble? Do You hold back because You know that as long as we think we can handle it we are deaf to Your offers of help?

I really know the answer—it is contained in the question. And because I know, today I can unequivocally say, "Thank you, Father, for my insomnia."

Wouldn't you like to feel thankful for yours, instead of fearful or full of self-pity? It can happen. You can know the joy of learning to praise God when you'd rather not, seeking out all the beatitudes hiding in the Bible that will bless your wakeful nights, asking, "Will I ever sleep again?" without fearing the answer, and exchanging your sleepless nights for adventures and discovery.

I'm ready to show you. Are you ready to learn?

References and Suggested Midnight Reading

1. H. Wayne Pipkin, *Christian Meditation: Its Art and Practice* (New York: Hawthorn Books, Inc., 1977).

2. Frank Laubach, *Channels of Spiritual Power* (Old Tappan, New Jersey: Fleming H. Revell Company, 1954).

Two ★

Getting Your Mind Off Self and On God

If God wanted to talk to you, could He get a word in edgewise? Could you hear Him above the clamor of worry in your head? Or is sleeplessness deafening you, sucking you down into a whirlpool of self-absorption?

Yes, sometimes it *can* seem as though everything in life depends on whether you will be able to sleep tonight. Tomorrow you may be starting a new job, or taking a crucial exam, or having the whole family over for holiday dinner. You may be a hotshot salesman priming for that sale of the century, or a pastor trying to write the ultimate sermon on stewardship. Whoever you are, if nightly you squander precious energy worrying about not sleeping until your nerves whine like violin strings wound one turn too many—read on.

Nonsleepers can grow deaf to God as they contend with unremitting physical pain, grief over a death, betrayal by a false friend, marriage killed by a stony heart, fear of growing old alone, or—one of the worst—vague apprehensions that have no focus.

Impotent to deal with their problems in the lonely night, nonsleepers eventually allow insomnia to paint dark circles around their days as well as their eyes. Soon their chronic complaints about not being able to sleep alienate them from family and friends; their isolation is complete.

Without meaning to, the nonsleeper has made a career of sleeplessness. How easy it becomes, because the literal bed no longer consoles, to lie back on others' sympathy; to seek comfort in self-pity. But others become bored with saying "There, there" and self-pity is treacherous, fevering the soul and inflaming the imagination with what-ifs and if-onlys. Self-pity makes worry fester.

What might be the opposite of self-pity—what is the most self-forgetting thing you can do? Might it not be praising God?

Think about this definition: "[Praise is] an expression of admiration and an ascribing of glory; the offering of grateful homage in words or song, as an act of worship to God."[1]

Another definition: In the *Bible Reader's Encyclopedia and Concordance*, a slim book with a mighty title and mightier insights, praise is defined as "an important element in religion and in the psychological life of the worshiper. Overconcentration on our own unworthiness and sin would lead to morbidity; the recognition of God's glory and the praise of His good works towards men is necessary for our psychological as well as our spiritual salvation."[2]

Listen, as you think about these definitions of praise. Perhaps you already hear God quietly calling:

> *Look in My Book—look in My Book.*
> *Quit worrying long enough to*
> *look in My Book.*

For best results, I suggest you look first in a concordance and list any verses having to do with sleep or rest. You might as well—you aren't sleeping anyway. Then look them up in a Bible translation of your own choice (I favor the Amplified Bible, which gives every nuance of meaning), and record those which speak to you, adding your thoughts about each in a loose-leaf notebook.

As you compile your observations about sleep and rest, let the assurances that God loves you trickle into your consciousness. Give free passage to any stirrings you have of appreciation, gratitude, and praise. If you don't "feel like it" yet, praise Him anyway. You may need to praise God precisely because you don't feel like doing so. The simple act of looking in God's Book and risking belief in His faithfulness, love, power, and trustworthiness has begun to move you off the dead center of "poor me."

Besides, you can learn about all the "blesseds" in the Bible. Did you know that the First Psalm begins with a beatitude? As in all the other beatitudes tucked away in unexpected corners of the Bible, this one promises great blessings (happinesses) to the person who obeys God, gives Him praise, and waits for Him to point to the right path. The dictionary defines a *beatitude* as "a declaration of exalted happiness." All of us could use some of this from God.

Study Psalm 1. Take it personally. Then look for other psalms, such as the Twenty-ninth, a solemn paean of praise exalting God's majesty and worship-worthiness. David urges us to "give to the

Lord the glory due to His name," doing it "in the beauty of holiness" (verse 2 AMP). He recommends the kind of set-apartness for God that offers the whole self, saying God is worthy of our most reckless adoration.

Enthralled by God's voice, David entreats us to listen as the Lord speaks to His creation, letting the tiniest insect as well as Man, Creation's crown, know that He is the LORD. The Psalmist declares that God's voice thunders and flashes forth forked lightning; His voice, in power and majesty, breaks the trees and splits the earth. All, even the Deluge, He brought about by His voice.

In the last verse of this psalm, when you might reasonably expect David to advise you to quake and cower before so mighty a God, he says, instead, that "the Lord will give [unyielding and impenetrable] strength to His people; the Lord will bless His people with peace" (AMP).

Truly, He is a God not to be understood through logic but to be praised and adored, thanked and loved, without reservation.

Now ponder this—the God whose voice breaks trees waits to talk to you and me, in the middle of the night. Selah (pause and calmly think of that).[3]

As you turn from your problem to the problem solver, who waits to take you through your sleeplessness to the other side of the valley of night shadows, His promise, recorded in Jeremiah 29:11 (AMP), will assure you of His friendship. "For I know the thoughts and plans that I have for you . . . for welfare and peace, and not for evil, to give you hope in your final outcome."

When you decide to offer to God as much of your trust as you can, your ability to trust Him will increase. Like the little girl whose father set her on a wall and coaxed her to jump into his arms, you learn to leap off the wall into your Father's waiting arms. She couldn't just half-believe her father would catch her, nor can you. Practice launching yourself out into the thin air of faith, believing that "underneath are the everlasting arms" ready to catch, comfort, and sustain you.

Transferring attention from self to God in this way can soon dissolve those knots of self-pity and quicken your awareness of grace. Your concordance becomes a road map, your destination clearly marked by verses about praise. Being alone or lonely or sleepless or in pain no longer seems so important. Reading the Bible becomes dialogue with someone not visible but undeniably present. In silent conversation, God surrounds you with His sheltering arms and you are able to ask, without being afraid of the answer, "Will I ever sleep again?"

Through Proverb 3, God answers, "When you lie down you shall not be afraid; yes, you shall lie down and your sleep shall be sweet" (verse 24).

But maybe you are skeptical about hearing God in your head. If so, try this: Today, as you go about your regular tasks, be alert to the many times you talk to yourself about what you are doing or planning to do, making decisions on the basis of discussion— even argument—you have with yourself. This is the original committee, or what children call "me, myself, and I." We all use this inner dialogue. Some of us verbalize it. Many others never know they do it. My husband is a constant verbalizer. When he asks a question of an empty room we know he is externalizing his thinking on some project; this is his private conversation with his internal committee.

God may choose to communicate with you, working from inside, using your voice of me, myself, and I. One way to know if God is talking to you is to listen to your own inner arguments about sleeplessness.

A message counseling fear or discouragement will not be from Him. A voice—sensed or heard—suggesting how worthwhile it would be to spend a few middle-of-the-night hours with Him would be typical of our loving Father. At the same time you are listening to this voice, you will be able to tell how attuned you are to the Lord. If your "me" argues that nothing but a sleeping pill will help, your "myself" wonders if there might be something good about being awake after all, and your "I" decides to give it a try, you can be pretty sure that the healing work God wants to do in you has begun.

Some cynics declare that God doesn't talk to people. They make fun of those who claim to hear Him by saying things like, "Your problem is you're a half-bubble off true."

But, to use a different colloquialism, these cynics are trying to "row with one oar out of the water." They circle impotently in their own sourness because they have not yet identified their own inner dialogue or acknowledged God's presence.

God *is* present—and often vocal.

Has it occurred to you yet that being awake at night could be fun? If you believe that not sleeping is a life-threatening condition, that may sound like an outrageous statement.

Consider the new research into sleep disorders. Deliberate deprivation of sleep, carried on under strict laboratory monitoring, did not ruin the health of volunteers who underwent the ordeal for a week, night and day. After being awakened every time they dozed off, they were finally allowed to sleep. They neither went crazy nor fell ill; only one night's sleep was needed to recover. One odd by-product of the experiments alerted researchers to another area to explore. When volunteers were again allowed to sleep they dreamed almost constantly, as though making up for lost time.

Another, more informal experiment involved a seventeen-year-old in San Diego, California, who, according to Dr. William Dement, "managed to spend 264 hours without sleeping (11 days and nights)."[4] This volunteer, too, felt completely restored after a twelve-hour sleep.

Once your fear of insomnia as a health wrecker is gone, you have assessed the label "insomniac" correctly, and are open to God's solution to your nightly dilemma, most of the fatigue and short temper, the fuzziness and dullness so typical of the worried nonsleeper disappears. Think what it would be like to *enjoy* your wakeful late hours.

Are you ready to put aside all the "poor me" scares and anxieties? If so, the next time you can't sleep, leave your bed promptly. This means: Note the time you turn off the light; if you are awake enough to see the clock face a half-hour later, get up. Go to a place where you can turn on a light, sit down, and make a list—no, brainstorm a list—of things you'd most like to do with these bonus hours.

(Here, a word of caution. For those whose favorite midnight pastime is making love, look out. Waking up your spouse for this purpose may be a momentary pleasure, but it is also selfish and may very well leave you more dissatisfied than if you had let him/her sleep. Besides, it really doesn't solve your insomnia problem.)

Midnight brainstorming is so relaxing—nobody is looking over your shoulder, finding fault with your ideas or interrupting. Certainly, God won't. You are free to be a child again.

Let's say that one secret, goofy ambition of yours is to fly to the moon. Actual space travel is not yet open to tourists, but a variation on the theme could be marvelous fun. Maybe your version of flying to the moon would be to write poetry or music in an off-the-earth mood. Or maybe you've always wanted to study astronomy, or write science fiction stories.

Start now—while it's quiet—to make your plans. Another idea: With earphones you could listen to music that has an outer space theme, such as *The Planets* by Gustav Holst.[5]

Claim the middle of the night as your exclusive property, a time when no demands can be made upon you that you don't want to make upon yourself. Invite God to be your midnight companion, offering each brainstorm to Him, asking how you can use it to delight Him.

The activity needn't be "religious," however. If you are attempting poetry, for instance, a thought from your heart about the call of the meadowlark on a sparkling spring morning, or about the limpid innocence of a baby's smile, will suffice. Read such poets as Gerard Manley Hopkins or Luci Shaw to stimulate your personal gropings toward expression. And if you are shy about writing poetry, here is additional incentive: When I asked William Stafford (Oregon's Poet Laureate), "How do you know when you've written a poem?" he answered, "When you say it is a poem."

As you get into the swing of using your insomnia, you may find that you require less sleep than you thought you had to have. The eight hours generally thought to be needed is actually too much for some "short sleepers." One respondent to a questionnaire reports how dull and sluggish she feels the next day if she gets more than five hours of sleep a night. Once her inner clock announces that she has slept long enough, she might as well get up and get busy—at four in the morning.

Work out your sleep schedule the same way, without regard for the "oughts" and "shoulds" of well-meaning friends. If you are a "lark," ready to retire soon after sundown, don't be alarmed if you also wake up with the larks. If you've had your sleep by 5:00 A.M., why try to sleep until seven? Early mornings can be bonus hours, too. A brisk walk or jog in the fresh morning air, before traffic exhaust dirties it, does wonders for your circulation. Or, if you don't care to leave the house, try "sitting out" as Jean Hersey describes this early-morning occupation:

> . . . on our terrace, in a little spot where the wind is absent and the sun shines down . . . we have a chaise lounge and cushions . . . I wrap the car robe around me from back to front to keep out rear drafts.
>
> Thus bundled, I enjoy a couple of hours in the sun . . . I sew . . . write letters . . . always watch the birds . . . sometimes I just experience that enviable state of doing nothing . . . a lovely interlude of merely being . . . outdoors with the cold, cold air on your face . . . when you come in your skin glows and you feel a tingle . . . I seem to bring it (the outdoors) into the house with me.[6]

Deep within you and me is a God-imprinted need to be in touch with nature daily, and through it, with Him. The freshness of the early morning can sharpen your senses of being and of place as described by Hersey. No better antidote exists for the squirrel-in-the-cage feeling modern living inflicts. Once you have sat, warmly wrapped, in a quiet outside corner, observing the setting of the moon in the western quadrant at the same time you note the slow, steady lightening of the eastern sky, the phrase "communing with nature" will forever be rescued from banality. As you listen to the predawn bird concert and wonder why they fall silent just before the sun appears, you feel an even greater lift in your spirit as they burst into their joyous second chorus, heralding the new day. Now is the moment to have your Bible in hand, reading what another "sitter outer" had to say about the God who:

> . . . *called up the dawn* [and showed] *the morning its place . . .* [who] *taught it to grasp the fringes of the earth and shake the Dog-star from its place; to bring up the horizon in relief as clay under a seal, until all things stand out like the folds of a cloak, when the light of the Dog-star is dimmed and the stars of the Navigator's Line go out one by one. . . .*[7]

As you sit entranced by this daily wonder, you may recall how G. K. Chesterton mused that God is like children, who "have such abounding vitality, because they are in spirit fierce and free," that "they want things repeated and unchanged."[8]
Chesterton says:

> They always say, "Do it again"; and the grown-up person does it again until he is nearly dead. For grown-up people are not strong enough to exult in monotony. Perhaps God is strong enough . . . it is possible that God says every morning . . . "Do it again" to the sun . . . it may be that He has the eternal appetite of infancy. . . . Our Father is younger than we.[9]

If you smile and nod with recognition as you read this, then you are a natural "sitter outer," ready to applaud the secret daily encore God demands of the sun. You can thank Him that you were present and young enough to "exult in monotony."

With all this in mind, we can now see what we miss when we hug the viper of self-pity so close we poison our ability to receive God's blessings. But once we shift from self-absorption to soaking up little daily joys such as the sunrise, and life, and breath, and people, we are on the way to wholeness. Praise, first offered as a mechanical, awkward exercise of the will, becomes easier. Then, as we begin to believe God loves us, thanksgiving flows freely. Before we have time to wonder if we know how, we move into petition and intercessory prayer, the spontaneous response of our souls to Him. This is the antivenom given to cure our ills, bringing the peace that invites true rest—and perhaps sleep.

Have you brainstormed your list of favorite bonus-hour activities? Here is mine:

1. *Form a Happy Insomniacs Club.* Share ideas with other nonsleepers. What do they do when they can't sleep—not to get back to sleep but instead of sleeping? Advertise in your church newsletter for others interested in a Late Night Prayer Support Group, a Night Owls for God Club, or a Wee Hours Prayer Chain.

2. *Join Prison Fellowship.* Write to Charles Colson requesting the name of a prisoner who needs a friend. Use your bonus time to write a letter or to pray for that prisoner. Colson constantly pleads for more people to join the fellowship. Think of ways to spread the word about Prison Fellowship. Organize a local group among other insomniacs. Write to your state's prison or to the county facility. Explain your interest in helping prisoners and mention

Prison Fellowship.[10] If you are not familiar with Colson's mission to the prisoners, read his books.[11]

3. *Find an insomniac buddy* who will also be your midnight prayer partner. Agree on a phone signal, such as a single ring, to be used by either on wide-awake nights. The one called will not be disturbed if asleep; if awake he/she will know it is the other wakeful one calling. Use the time on the phone to remind each other that insomnia is an opportunity. Agree on your own prayer needs and prayer for others. Chat about anything mutually pleasant and agreeable.

4. *Start a scrapbook* about insomnia. Clip cartoons, bright quips, anecdotes, jokes, bits of philosophy or poetry. Title one section, "A funny thing happened to me last night when I couldn't sleep . . ." and record your thoughts, discoveries, and insights about insomnia, or incorporate this into your midnight journal.

5. *Watch for mention of insomnia by famous people* in newspaper or television interviews, profiles, and biographies. Write to them and encourage them to try your late-night brainstorms that help you enjoy being awake. They may ignore your letter, but you might gain a new friend and help someone master insomnia without the use of drugs. At the same time, you could witness to the reality of God as your best Friend.

These are only a few ideas—you probably have better ones. But whether or not you try brainstorming, do accept wide-awake or fast-asleep times equally as gifts from the God who gives both.

Apply the same principle you use when offering prayer for others. If you are like me, you are keenly aware of your own fallibility, so you keep a humble attitude toward knowing what is best for the object of your prayers. Rather than praying for a specific action or event, you might want to pray, "Whatever You know this person needs, Lord, let it be done."

Then, if you feel so led, you can pray, "Lord, help me know how to pray for this person according to Your will." If you know from Scripture what God has already said is His will (example: God would have all people be saved), then you can confidently pray in specifics. Or, if you get an unmistakable insight, pray according to your guidance. But knowing without a doubt what definite requests should be made happens far less often than some zealous prayer warriors would like to think.

Approach your wakeful times with this same humility. Allow some room for a different opinion—God's—as to how you should be using the night. You could be frustrating His good intentions for you by refusing to accept wakefulness as a blessing. The Bible says that God has a secret "framed from the very beginning."[12]

Yes, God has His reasons—but one towers above all others, a reason involving His very nature and your whole future. In the next chapter we will find out what it is.

References and Suggested Midnight Reading/Listening

1. *The Random House Dictionary of the English Language*, unabridged edition (New York: Random House, 1973).

2. W. M. Clow, D.D., *The Bible Reader's Encyclopedia and Concordance*, revised edition (London–New York: Collins Clear-Type Press, 1962).

3. Translation of *Selah* in The Amplified Bible (Grand Rapids, Michigan: Zondervan Publishing House, 1965).

4. William C. Dement, M.D., *Some Must Watch While Some Must Sleep* (New York: W. W. Norton & Co., Inc., 1976).

5. Gustav Holst, *The Planets*, Eugene Ormandy, conductor,

RCA. Or the same piece, Leonard Bernstein, conductor, Columbia.

6. Jean Hersey, *The Touch of the Earth* (San Francisco: Seabury Press, 1981).

7. Job 38:12–15, The New English Bible (New York: Oxford University Press, Cambridge University Press, 1970).

8. G. K. Chesterton, "The Ethics of Elfland," *Orthodoxy* (New York: Doubleday & Co., Inc., 1959).

9. Ibid.

10. *Jubilee,* the Newsletter of Prison Fellowship.
> Charles Colson
> P.O. Box 17500
> Washington, D.C. 20041

11. Charles Colson, *Born Again* (Old Tappan, New Jersey: Fleming H. Revell Company, 1977). Also *Life Sentence*, same publisher, 1981.

12. First Corinthians 2:8 NEB. See also Ephesians 3:9 AMPLIFIED.

Three ★ _____
God
Has His
Reasons

"But why?" I would ask Mother.

"Because I say so," she would reply patiently. "I have my reasons. Just do as you're told, and we'll discuss it later."

Somehow we never discussed it later. Once I'd grudgingly done whatever it was she wanted, the *why* lost its importance.

Of course, that didn't prevent me from "whying" her the next time I felt rebellious. And thus I grew—and learned about the wisdom of parental strategy.

I've also learned, as a result of my insomnia, about my divine Parent's patience, as deep flowing as my mother's but with an added dimension hers lacked. Inevitably, her forbearance dried up; His is inexhaustible.

During those long, wakeful nights, once I'd learned to listen, I began to wonder why God never gives up on us, His balky, stubborn children, the way human parents do. His Book held the answer while He waited for me to grow up enough to see it.

The Lord has the most powerful reason imaginable, one that proceeds from His very nature: He has committed Himself to finish what He started. As Paul told the Philippians, "I am convinced . . . that He Who began a good work in you will continue . . . bringing it to full completion in you."[1]

Thus, our Father works patiently with and in us to help us become the selves He intends us to be. True to His purpose, He stands quietly in the background as we blunder through life, empathizing with every bruise as we bounce off the stone walls of experience. He bides His time; He waits for us to realize we can't cope alone; He waits for us to turn to Him for the help He yearns to give. And yet, He allows us trial and error, not sheltering us entirely from the pain of growing up.

To some degree, we all have chafed against the rules and regulations our parents make, longing in our immaturity for the imagined time when we will fling off the "chains" of childhood. Oh frabjus day when we will become adults! It's as though we think we will be issued a cosmic credit card. Very soon after, of course, we learn the harsh truth that if we want the amenities we must pay our bills. If we crave companionship or love and marriage, we must become the person another will want for a friend or a spouse. When this insight occurs, our parents' long-term goal for us comes into sight at last.

We do our spiritual growing up in much the same way. Events can happen, however, that at first glance dismay us. How can losing a job, watching parents get old and die, suffering through endless sleepless nights be good for us? How can "bad things happening" be creative? How can God use negative circumstances to achieve His purposes? The first time this was suggested to me I simply rejected it out of hand, totally misapprehending the uses of adversity. Leslie Weatherhead changed my mind.

Have you noticed how God is always being blamed for disasters, accidents, untimely deaths? Insurance companies traditionally cover all bases by including an "act of God" rider in policies, compounding the universal assumption that He causes calamities.

Weatherhead dispersed my anxieties by explaining, through concise identifications of the three main dimensions of God's will, how God's hands-off love works.

Those dimensions are: Intentional, Circumstantial, and Ultimate.[2] For your midnight reading I recommend his little classic, *The Will of God*, which shows so clearly that God is like the horse tamer who seeks to harness rather than to break a wild creature's spirit. Through the grace of His Circumstantial Will, God shows us it is possible to be in the midst of trouble but untroubled. To achieve this, He calls to us constantly, sometimes right through our distraction over insomnia. Do we listen—or resist listening?

If we turn a deaf ear to God, it might be because He always seems to be calling us to impossible tasks. If He isn't requiring us to agree with Him that we are sinners, or to love our enemies, He's wanting us to be glad we have insomnia. Is this reasonable? And if we do hear Him, however inadvertently, we act as though He'd asked us to step into a fiery furnace or to sacrifice a child. That's odd, the Bible tells about His servants who willingly did exactly that—and lived to enjoy a more intimate friendship with Him because they were obedient. And they didn't ask why.[3]

Accustomed as we are to thinking of these people as giants of faith, we forget that God was "growing them up," too, to fulfill His purposes for them in the same way He wants to fulfill His purposes in us. Yes, God has His reasons, often hidden in the very circumstances we call bad.

For instance, if you have been sleepless five or six nights in a row, do you consider it a crisis? Are you planning to use sleeping pills to knock yourself out at the next hint of sleeplessness, or are you more likely to offer your insomnia to God, asking Him what He wants you to do with it?

Are you complaining that not being able to sleep isn't fair when you work so hard for the Lord, or have you decided to enroll in God's night school because there may be something here to learn?

Do you see getting back to sleep as your only worthwhile goal, or are you ready to listen to His reasons you should be awake?

A questionnaire was sent to a random sampling of people willing to respond to the query "What do you do about your insomnia?" You may wish to compare your own experiences.

Case A "I've Tried Everything"

One insomniac who seldom gets more than four consecutive hours of sleep per night tried sleeping pills, hot milk, honey and vinegar, herbs, homeopathic medicine, calcium and magnesium oratate, tryptophan,[4] reading, prayer, reciting Scripture, relaxation tapes, getting up and working until sleepy, counseling—no improvement.

"Sometimes," she admitted, "it helps to get up and write out my feelings and thoughts in my journal."

Case A, convinced that "dreams are one important way God communicates with us . . . and necessary for mental health" feels deprived and dead-ended. Most of her sleep stays in the alpha or lightest sleep state, seldom descending into the deep delpha state so necessary if she is to achieve the shift from non-REM to REM sleep, where most dreaming occurs. (In *Creative Insomnia*, Douglas Colligan describes this process in vivid detail.[5])

Deprived of dream fellowship with her Lord, her health in seeming jeopardy, she can't figure out how to get to sleep and solve her problem. The Bible, which once brought her great peace and comfort, no longer does so, adding to her spiritual distress.

Nevertheless, Case A leaves herself in God's hands, waiting ". . . for Him to show His goodness by some other means, because He does care about me—totally."

For such wakeful, hopeful insomnia victims as Case A, chapter 9 offers a simple alternative that can solve the double problem of sleeplessness/dream deprivation at the same time it enriches spiritual life.

Case B "My Mind Won't Quit"

This young man, responsible for a growing family, attending college, participating in athletics, and working part-time, is so on the go during the day he can't stop at night. An insomniac since childhood, he's given up analyzing why he had it so early and now simply tries—unsuccessfully—to deal with his present sleeplessness. He reports:

I try consciously to clear my mind and relax my body, or I may stay up and read or pray. No one thing has ever really helped all the time. . . . I have tried praying in a variety of ways . . . sometimes I ask God for sleep, or for help to relax, or to resolve a thought pattern positively. At other times, I ask for strength simply to praise Him . . . it seems to help. . . . The act of turning an idea over to God . . . may have provided the release I needed. . . .

He adds, "I find that the Lamentations make me realize the relative insignificance of my daily irritations [but really] my only hope is that God loves and touches me."

Since Case B already has sought help in the Bible, he also may feel comfortable with chapter 9. Exercise #5, on transposing the Bible into your own key, details new ways to find hope and help.

Case C "I Claim His Promise"

The third sampling shows a sleepless person who has begun to realize that getting back to sleep may not hold top priority after all. For her, striving for sleep is beginning to give way to acceptance, an attitude all insomniacs should seek. She says that her solution for insomnia "depends on what is causing it":

For tension or stress I take a warm bath . . . read, exercise, drink warm milk at bedtime. If the problem seems to be spiritual, I ask God through prayer what it is and seek His help to map out a plan of action. But if it is none of these things, I claim one of His promises regarding sleep, usually, "For so he giveth his beloved sleep."[6]

And yet, like so many others, she assumes that getting back to sleep is the key and the solution. She will find, in chapter 4, "As

Long as I'm Up, Lord . . .", the fresh approach she needs to draw the fangs of insomnia.

Serenity and a Sense of Humor: A Conclusion

Why do some wakeful persons panic at not being able to get back to sleep while others remain unafraid? Why will one say, "I don't actually pray for the ability to sleep . . . I do pray for help with problems that keep me awake, placing them in God's hands," while another lies wide-eyed in the dark, trapped in worry?

Each of the cases reported shows a natural desire to retrieve the mislaid knack of sleeping. None view insomnia as *opportunity*. If they pray, it is for sleep. Wakefulness is something to escape from; sleep becomes a handy rabbit hole of refuge.

Next, however, we will look at a person who has taken into account the possibility that God has His reasons for allowing or even for causing insomnia—and is not alarmed.

Case D "Why Not Laugh at Insomnia?"

Case D, who has lived with insomnia for more than ten years, reports, "I haven't fought my insomnia but instead use it as an extra time for concentrated thinking . . . I prefer to look upon it as an opportunity rather than a liability."

This nonsleeper is also one of the few who keeps her sense of humor intact in the face of sleepless nights. A "Peanuts" fan, she enclosed the following two Charles Schulz cartoon strips with her response to the questionnaire:

Reprinted by permission of United Feature Syndicate, Inc.

Being able to laugh at insomnia actually relaxes the defenses of secret resentment we erect against God for allowing or causing our insomnia. Because Case D has made herself available to God through her sense of humor, she hasn't far to go to gain control of it. Later in her answers to the questionnaire, she further reveals her philosophy of dealing with sleeplessness.

When I can't sleep I try to evaluate what might have transpired during the day to contribute to it. Praying and getting up to read often helps. As for personal problems, after years of fruitless struggle I've learned to give them to God . . . it is so futile to wrestle all night in the dark. . . .

Case D will probably find much that is familiar in chapter 5, "What *Is* Rest, Really?" because she has already begun to understand how to rest whether or not she sleeps.

★

Sleep, like all other benefits of life, is a gift from God. Who can challenge His right to withhold or bestow sleep on the grounds that we don't understand His reasons? I suggest that although most insomniacs never doubt they have a right to sleep, now is the time to relinquish that right. We must eschew the frame of mind typical of most insomniacs. One correspondent wrote, "I find it very upsetting to think that God might disturb my sleep. I don't know that God does any such thing."

Apparently, insomnia as a manifestation of a chronic spiritual problem bothered him greatly. He declared that he would not be pleased to be awakened regularly until the alleged problem between him and God was resolved.

But demanding as a right the ability to sleep, or objecting to being awakened in the middle of the night—for whatever reason—seems inconsistent for the Christian. In other situations do we not defer to God, trusting His reasons, whether hidden or apparent?

Nobody likes to be awakened in the night, but what if God knows we *need* to be awakened—one, two, or twenty nights in a row—so He can help us identify and admit our spiritual ills, and then heal them for us? Isn't this insomnia situation also one in which we should defer to His wisdom? Any time a Christian says, "Father, I'd rather do it myself," he/she is in trouble.

In today's jargon we would say that making demands is "contraindicated." George MacDonald describes the only demand the human creature can make upon God. In *Creation in Christ*,[7] the condensed version of MacDonald's classic, *Unspoken Sermons*,[8] he reveals what he calls "the greatest discovery of all": ". . . God owes Himself to the creature He has made in His

51

image, for so He has made him incapable of living without Him. This . . . is His divinest gift to them. For the fulfilling of this claim, He has sent His son. . . ."

Once our perspective about demands is restored, we give up the absurdity that declares, "Now, God, this is what I have a right to do, and here are my plans. So just countersign my blueprint here at the bottom, below my own signature, if You will, please."

Instead, our good sense restored, we acquiesce, "Lord, You have Your reasons, and they are better than mine. I want to do whatever You want me to do."

Then comes the wonderful benefit of giving in to God. Although mothers aren't always right when they say, "Do it because I say so," God can be trusted to be right 100 percent of the time.

Once convinced of God's utter trustworthiness, the insomniac finds a new attitude of "Now what?" taking shape. In the next chapter, this life-changing way of looking will be explored.

References and Suggested Midnight Reading

1. Philippians 1:6 AMPLIFIED.

2. Leslie Weatherhead, *Will of God* (Nashville: Abingdon Press, 1944).

According to Weatherhead, God's will is no more to be broken up into three different wills than the Trinity is to be thought of as three different gods. On the contrary, God's will is like a sparkling gem of many facets. That simile is best used by saying the three main facets are:

Intentional Will (God's original plan for our well-being and happiness)

Circumstantial Will (God's temporary plan in the midst of evil-dominated circumstances)

Ultimate Will (God's final realization of His original plan, which nothing can defeat)

3. Shadrach, Meshach, and Abednego in Daniel 3:12–30; Abraham in Genesis 22.

4. Douglas Colligan, *Creative Insomnia* (New York: McGraw-Hill Book Company, 1978), pp. 91–93. Colligan says the following:

Tryptophan is a natural protein found in a variety of foods, from peanut butter to steak. [It] provides the raw material for a brain chemical, serotin, which sleep researchers now know is a prime ingredient needed to switch on the sleep centers in the brain. (Milk is another good source.)

5. Ibid., pp. 8–10.

Author Colligan explains in detail what happens when a person sleeps. He says, "Your whole system is in an orderly state of commotion during sleep and at any given time is either moving down away from or up towards wakefulness . . . even before you lie down in bed your brain is already shifting gear. . . ."

6. Psalms 127:2 KJV.

7. George MacDonald, *Creation in Christ*, condensed by Roland Heim (Wheaton, Illinois: Harold Shaw Publishers, 1976).

8. George MacDonald, *Unspoken Sermons*. Out-of-print Volumes I, II, III (1870, 1884, 1891).

Four ★ _____

As Long
as I'm Up,
Lord ...

Now you no longer need to fight your insomnia. Free to explore God's intentions, you are ready to say to Him, "Now what?"

This may not be what you decide to do. Old habits are hard to break. That first impulse to try to recapture sleep, the unreasoning panic that seemed to threaten your very life, does not simply go away once you've decided to put wakefulness to work. The weight of societal opinion that says you must sleep at night is heavy indeed. Why else the perennially brisk sales of "sure cure" sleep retrieval manuals, medications, sleep-aid commercials, if sleep isn't vital?

Thus, people who regard being awake at night merely as an interesting break in their routine must be considered odd and out-of-step.

Of course, there are those who belong to the night owl crowd, whose inner clocks normally schedule wide-awakeness when others are asleep. They feel quite comfortable with it. Thomas Edison is said to have invented the electric light to spare himself eyestrain during his late-night experiments.

On a recent "NOVA" program which explored sleep patterns, one middle-aged English man testified that he could get along just fine on *one hour of sleep per night*. He's been doing it for years and said he couldn't see wasting more time than that on sleeping.

And you, a veteran of the insomnia war, know how strong the cultural conditioning is for you to concentrate on getting back to sleep. Yet sleep, like happiness, does not yield to pursuit. Instead, the solution comes indirectly, a vision seen out of the corner of your eye.

Ask yourself if you have been like the tunnel-visioned insomniac whose late-night encounter with God revolutionized his life but who then said, "There—I've got my life all straightened out with You, Lord—*now* can I get some sleep?" He just didn't understand.

If this scenario sounds familiar, you may also know about those thoughts that bounce around like Ping-Pong balls:

How do I do it—sleep, that is?
What is sleep, anyway?
What if I've forgotten how?
Maybe something else is wrong with me. . . .

The next thing you know, your old enemy, fear, gets a grip on you again, and your body cooperates by supplying those little twinges here and tiny stabs of pain there. Once again your heartbeat becomes eerily audible, with strange hesitations and subbeats. You find it impossible to lie still, your legs get the fidgets, your pillow hardens, the covers wrap themselves demonically around your body. You try to pray but it's like fighting with a paper sword.

At last, unable to remain in bed, you get up and prowl the house, frightening yourself by reading an intruder into ordinary creaks and settlings any house goes through at night. You check and recheck door and window locks; you might even look in on other sleepers, padding restlessly through dark rooms and halls.

Old fears and regrets pounce on your imagination as you sort mentally through lost loves, missed chances, unfulfilled ambitions. Guilt, so recently tossed on the garbage heap, leaps to life in a new guise:

> Why didn't I . . . ?
> If only I had . . .
> I never should have . . .
> I can never forgive myself for . . .

As this gloomy cavalcade marches by, adrenaline, answering the alarm set off by your fears, rushes along your bloodstream, forcing you ever more awake. Sleep is a lost cause once again, as lost as the Ten Tribes of Israel. Staring into the dark, you watch the clock tick off the hours. Unthinkingly, you have fallen back into the trap of believing your life depends on sleep.

See how programmed we are to this notion, how vulnerable we are because we believe it in spite of the evidence? One sleep expert, Dr. Dietrich Langen, declares, "Sleep is of no concern;

rest is important," and suggests some self-hypnotic procedures for obtaining rest. He recommends that the insomniac try for "as much indifference as possible to being awake, to neutralize the sleep disturbance."[1]

But self-hypnosis will never give the peace-filled rest that comes with listening, first to God "in the silent night" and then to the messages one's own being—body/mind/spirit—sends.

Amazing creation, the human being. God equips it with everything necessary to live well, including the ability to listen to Him and to the inner, unique self. With the ear tuned to positive messages you can learn to rest, awake, if you refuse to let it bother you that you are not sleeping. If you are one of the thirty million people in the United States who, according to Dr. William Dement (*Psychology Today*, June 1986), struggle with the chronic disorder of initiating and maintaining sleep called DIMS, that's better news than a telegram announcing you are a winner of the lottery. (Dr. Dement is a major sleep disorder researcher and psychiatrist at the University of California at Stanford's "mother" sleep lab, where sleep lab technicians go for training.)

Whatever happens to you now is almost wholly dependent on you and your day-by-day choices and decisions. God does not set us on a rigid track of His choice—He does not have one plan only for each of us, to run on willy-nilly or be derailed forever. Free will, within boundaries God alone perceives, gives us the right to make decisions, to take action, to move onward. We can make mistakes, go down wrong roads and, as Martin Luther says, ". . . sin boldly, but believe and rejoice in Christ even more boldly . . . pray boldly—you too are a mighty sinner."[2] From out of the mysterious tension of God's purpose for us:

We are assured and know that [God being a partner in their labor], all things work together and are [fitting into a plan] for good to those who love God and are called according to [His] design and purpose.[3]

Leaning confidently against the strong stretch fabric of free will, you can ask God to be senior partner in your quest for meanings, whether awake or asleep. As soon as you give up blaming sleeplessness on those who cause you worry, no longer attribute your insomnia to a medical problem, no longer plead advanced age, or the condition of the world, or any other predicament of our race, but look inside yourself, answers will emerge. *He* is in there, as well as "out there," in the Person of the Holy Spirit. If you believe that your body/mind/spirit is the temple of the Holy Spirit, then it is reasonable to seek His advice and counsel within that temple.

Practicality and spirituality are *not* mutually exclusive. You can be spiritually inclined at the same time you deal with your insomnia in a down-to-earth manner. Because something very simple may be causing your sleeplessness, you may wish to test the following suggestions of things *not* to do when you can't sleep:

Do Not

Take tranquilizers or sleeping pills
Lie in bed sleepless, staring into the dark, worrying
Watch late-night television
Wake up someone to share your misery
Drink anything other than water, warm milk, herbal tea
Console yourself with food
Label yourself an insomniac to get sympathy

On the other hand, you might try these things to *do* when you can't sleep:

Do

Engage in brisk exercise every day: jogging, racquetball, softball, swimming, tennis, gardening, chasing Frisbees, bicycling, walking

These suggestions have two purposes: (1) to show you inequities or stress-causing activities that contribute to insomnia, and (2) to narrow your options to one possibility.

Having checked off all the do's and don'ts, are you still having trouble sleeping? Then consider yourself a candidate for the exciting opportunity hidden in your insomnia. Now is the time to ask God, "As long as I'm up, Lord . . . what would *You* have me do?"

Recurring insomnia may be God's signal that He not only wants to talk to you about the way your life is going but also about your future service to Him.

Since sleeping is turning out to be *not* the most important event of your night, find out what *is*. The next night you can't sleep, abandon all attempts at retrieval and anticipate a fresh adventure instead. When your inner self complains that you must get up in a few hours and go to work, or care for children, or go to school for that big exam, quietly agree that these are legitimate demands while you make a self-to-self pact never again to put yourself through an anxiety binge about not sleeping.

In chapter 2, you were invited to brainstorm your own late-night activities. Here, your first move is to go outside. Find a comfortable nook or cranny where you can enjoy the night.

Bundle up, if necessary, and sit on the porch, patio, balcony or steps, or by an open window where you can relax and be ready for whatever you will see or hear.

Listen—get reacquainted with the night personality of wherever you live. If it's raining, stay under shelter, cultivating that cozy feeling of hearing rain when you needn't be out in it. Feel the wind, look for stars or the moon, listen as a solitary airplane drones overhead. Let yourself hear how different night sounds are from day sounds. As you sit quietly, note the mystery of familiar shapes changed by the night or by moonshine. Taste the night air with nose and tongue; notice the freshness given off by trees or a passing rain shower.

Then, think of all the people on your side of the world, asleep while you are awake. Or think of people also awake who are in pain or in trouble. Encourage the rising protective feeling for them within yourself; think of yourself as a watchman guarding the wall of the world. If you hear the wail of a siren, send a little prayer winging after that ambulance or police car.

Now let this train of thought go a bit further. Let it bring to mind special persons in your life and invite good, upbeat thoughts about them to flow. You may find this to be the first time in years you have done other than take them for granted, or to have other than a faultfinding attitude toward them. Even if you always think kindly toward them, try this as a pump primer:

> . . . *all that is true, all that is noble, all that is just and pure, all that is lovable and gracious [of good repute], whatever is excellent and admirable—fill all your thoughts [of those special persons] with these things.*

Philippians 4:8 NEB

It's a peculiar fact of life that most of us are kinder to strangers—not to mention more polite—than to our mother, father, spouse, sister, brother, or child. Think of the many ways those dear to you enrich your life. Whether they are close family or good friends, recall happy times with them; savor little character quirks they have that make you smile to remember.

If your impulse now is to pray for certain ones, first thank God for bringing them into your life. Then pray that God will surround them with His love. One at a time, visualize each in the center of a white radiance, bathed in God's blessing, love, and protection. As you do this, ask God to do for him/her whatever He knows is needed. You might pray that the person will be given a sense of God's comforting presence.

For the moment, put aside thoughts about unfinished projects, unsatisfactory relationships, or career disappointments. If such thoughts persist, quietly give them to God, asking for His peace. Remember that every time you depend on God for strength you reinforce your future ability to believe in and trust Him.

We have often heard it said that in the early hours, from two until dawn, our resistance is low, both spiritually and physically. Medical people and clergy alike say that those hours before the dawn are times when many of the dying expire, slipping away because the life force flickers at its lowest point. During those fragile hours, we seem most vulnerable to depression; we don't think as clearly or as purposefully as during the day. Perhaps the existential loneliness of every human being, held at bay by the bustle of daily life, overwhelms our defenses at night by rushing into the vacuum daytime distractions fill.

Whatever the reason, our very defenselessness, which unbars

the door to the enemy, also opens it to our best Friend, God. So let yourself be vulnerable to Him; trust Him as much as you are able. If you will risk admitting your weakness in those early hours He can do great things in your life. He knows how inadequate you feel. He understands your fears and your aloneness, so ask Him what you should do.

★

Here you are, then, outside in the night, your attention focused on special persons. You have provided yourself a chance to examine in detail what they mean to you and to God. Go over your relationships, talking to God and listening for His replies. Practice honesty, sweeping aside facades you've erected to protect yourself from the truth. Ask yourself if you habitually distance yourself from those others, effectively blocking intimacy. How do you treat people? How do you handle day-to-day encounters?

Think now . . . is there a rift or a coldness between you and another? Dare to ask God what to do about it. Resist the impulse to defend or rationalize your actions and feelings. You've done what you've done; you feel what you feel. Acknowledge these acts and feelings; resist shifting the blame from yourself to the other person.

Seek to advance from a grudging "Maybe I could have been a little nicer" to "I know I'm sometimes impatient with her" to "Show me, Lord, how to love her with Your love, for I have been unkind and unfair.'" (Wrestling Jacoblike with one such relationship per session is quite enough.)

Trust the conviction that God has allowed or planned this wakeful situation for therapeutic reasons. He knows that before you can become an intercessor—every Christian is called to be one—you must first inventory your life. Spouse, parents, chil-

dren, intimate friends—all the closest who know you best—
should be brought forward in your mind, one by one, so you can
examine what is good and not so good between you. Jesus said it
so well:

> So if, when you are offering your gift at the altar you there
> remember that your brother has any [grievance] against you,
> Leave your gift at the altar and go; first make peace with your
> brother, and then come back and present your gift.[4]

Making peace with those who matter most to you must occur
before the peace of God can fill your life with intercessory power.
Many an otherwise exemplary Christian, bathed in the warm
glow of others' high opinion, carries a fatal flaw. He has allowed
a rift between himself and a friend, or his child, or his spouse, to
widen into an abyss of alienation. Perhaps in other aspects of his
life he has scrupulously obeyed God's ordinances, but in this one
instance stubborn pride says he is right and the other person is
wrong, separating him from God as by a high wall. (This
example is equally true using "she.")

As William Barclay observes:

> We sometimes wonder why there is a barrier between us and God
> . . . our prayers unavailing . . . we ourselves have erected that
> barrier . . . we have wronged someone and have done nothing to
> put things right.[5]

Humbling oneself under God's hand, being willing to repent,
seeking God's healing of a relationship, hungering above all to be
right with God—these steps you must take before you can go back

to the altar where your gift of yourself (What would You have me do, Lord?) waits to be presented to God with clean hands.

As much as these sessions in the fresh night air will increase your enjoyment of God's night, their main intent is to bring you into focus with Him. God uses your wakefulness or He awakens you, not to torment you or to amuse Himself but to enlist you in His army of pray-ers.

Do you resist such recruitment? Are you reluctant to commit yourself? Maybe it is extremely inconvenient to be stripped of comforting defenses that insulate your ego against the cold winds of examination. You may think:

> Don't I have any rights?
> Even You, God, have to admit that the one I called friend has treated me abominably . . . my not getting the job because what's-his-name knew how to stroke the boss was grossly unfair . . . that professor really hates me . . . nobody appreciates me—I'm just a meal ticket around here. . . .

And what has all this to do with insomnia? That's just the point. God *always* goes to your most tender spot. Whatever is keeping you awake is precisely where He wants to clean house. Those sample situations may have nothing to do with your particular dilemma, but your problem, whatever it is, is keeping you from sleeping or is waking you up, isn't it? Unsolved, unconfronted, it may also be causing headaches, stiff neck, back trouble, indigestion, palpitations, even arthritis and skin irritations, erosion of inner peace, chronic bitterness, and a sour disposition.

How about waiving your rights instead of waving your rights?

Someone has wisely said, "If what you're doing doesn't work, try something else."

Such simple advice. But if you are lying awake night after night, your eyes burning with lack of sleep and your heart burning with growing resentment against the unfairness of it all, isn't it time to try God's simple way?

Now reconciliation between you and God is an accomplished fact at last, right? (You have, after all, "learned to listen in the silent night.") So why isn't it?

Not to worry. We seldom learn God's lessons the first time He teaches them. As supreme Teacher, He understands this and makes allowances for our thickheadedness. So although it seems inconsistent that having met God in the night, confessed your sins, and begun again with a clean slate, you still detect anger, bitterness, and bewilderment at the perversity of life roiling inside you, don't despair. The Lord will not flunk you out of His school because you are a slow learner. He will teach you the same lesson as many times as you need to learn it. Assurance of His loving-kindness and patience are best demonstrated in His Book. Look, for instance, at one passage in the Psalms:

> *As a father loves and pities his children, so the Lord loves and pities those who fear Him. . . . For He knows our frame; He [earnestly] remembers and imprints [on His heart] that we are dust.*[6]

Giving up your "rights"—even if it means swimming upstream against society's obsession with doing your own thing—can be your best move.

All this is prep school. Now for the hard part:

You have let go of your autonomy, but now you must go to the person with whom you seek a healed relationship. God says you are to tell that person you have realized you are not blameless in the alienation. Asking someone to forgive you is not a thing you safely attempt in your own strength. You must go claiming the "spirit . . . of power, and of love, and of a sound mind," rejecting the paralyzing spirit of fear.[7]

Then comes the shock. You've said, "Please forgive me," only to have someone shrug and reply, "It's nothing," or "Forget it—I have." The person implies that the occasion was unimportant; absolution and forgiveness are unimportant; therefore, *you* are unimportant. Being trivialized thus is shattering. You may now feel worse than when your broken relationship was keeping you awake nights.

Or you receive another kind of shock. The person who rejects your plea either distances himself from you with silence or declares brutally, "I can't forgive you. What you did was unforgivable."

How we long for the ideal, the lovely moment when forgiveness reunites us with tears and hugs or the strong handgrip and eye contact that means the friendship is healed. Now the bond between you will be even stronger, like a broken bone thicker at the point of healing because the body has rushed a special order of calcium to the break.

But because life doesn't always work out that well, here is a contingency plan for moments when forgiveness is refused.

Once you have sought forgiveness, the responsibility shifts from your shoulders to God's—and to the person who refuses to forgive you. You made your move and were spurned. Will this, too, keep you up nights? Have you traded one worry for a worse one?

Now intercessory prayer comes into its own. Because you have met God's conditions, your fellowship with Him is intact. No further concern there. So instead of brooding about the injustice of not being forgiven, try tossing aside your hurt feelings the way you would discard a paper bag and, with love toughened by your own humbling, intercede for the unforgiving one.

What a divine joke! What a sense of euphoria dazzles your prayer life. You are free—free to pray that he will repent of his refusal. You are free to give up your feelings of injury. You are free to let agape love, the love that ignores slights and rebuffs and hurts, the love that persists "in spite of" as well as "because of"—Christ's own love—flood into your life and irresistibly into the life of the one who refuses to forgive.

How can mere sleep compete?

Expect this kind of breakthrough to take several sessions under the stars. If bad weather keeps you indoors, at least seek a location away from your bed/battlefield so you will not feel hampered by concern about waking others. Wrestling, after all, is not a quiet occupation.

What does God want you to do? He wants you to let Him show you how to bring your life into line with His will, to let Him reestablish His Fatherhood to your childship, to accept the easy yoke of Christ, who promises to make any burden light, to receive His forgiveness and to forgive yourself, and to seek forgiveness from others, freely granting it to them, too. He wants you to learn that even though another withholds forgiveness from you, peace can be yours by the bold act of forgiving the unforgiving, and then by interceding for the one who wants to remain your enemy.

Thus, to become an intercessor, you first take care of your own spiritual housecleaning, then pray for the blessing of those you love. Those first two lessons, introductory though they may seem, are vital for the next, more difficult one: to pray for your enemy. Anyone who resists reconciliation with you, by robbing you of your peace of mind and shaking your belief that you are your Father's child, becomes your enemy. But someone can *remain* your enemy only if you allow it. Jesus seems to ask the impossible when He commands, "Love your enemy," causing us to ask, "Why, Lord?"

Why, indeed, unless He knows that with His strength in us, and His mind in us, and His love blazing in us, we can get rid of an enemy without breaking a single one of God's laws—by changing that enemy into a friend.

If you are awake again tonight, try this: Ask God, "As long as I'm up, Lord . . . what would You have me do?" and let whatever happens from then on, happen.

References and Suggested Midnight Reading

1. Dietrich Langen, M.D., *Speaking of Sleeping Problems*, Medical Advisor Series (New York: Consolidated Book Publishers, 1978).

2. *Luther's Works*, Volume 48 (Philadelphia: Fortress Press, 1963), pp. 281, 282.
Martin Luther said in a letter to his friend Philip Melancthon on August 1, 1521:

If you are a preacher of grace, then preach a true and not a fictitious grace; if grace is true you must bear a true and not a fictitious sin. God does not save people who are only fictitious sinners. Be a sinner and sin boldly, but believe and rejoice in

Christ even more boldly, for He is victorious over sin, death and the world. . . . Do you think that the purchase price that was paid for the redemption of our sins by so great a Lamb is too small? Pray boldly—you too are a mighty sinner.

3. Romans 8:28 AMPLIFIED.

4. Matthew 5:23, 24 AMPLIFIED.

5. William Barclay, *The Daily Bible Study Series*, The Gospel of Matthew, Volume 2 (Philadelphia: Westminster Press, 1958).

6. Psalms 103:13, 14 AMP.

7. Second Timothy 1:7 KJV.

Five ★

What *Is* Rest, Really?

Whatever else happens when you ask God, "What would You have me do?" one event is predictable. You will gain insight into what rest is. Funny thing—as competently as we Americans deal with other things, we really don't know how to rest. The old joke about being glad to get home from vacation so we can rest up by going back to work has its roots in truth. If you took a quick poll, how many of your friends would reveal that they have to be sick before they can give themselves permission to read a book, stare out a window, idle away an hour without guilt?

Maybe you'd have to add your name to that list.

The panic some insomniacs feel when they can't sleep at night may come from an equally mistaken assumption. Being asleep at night is an acceptable occupation of the night hours, but being awake is not. So when insomniacs are not sleeping they feel they are violating some unwritten law, even when their sleeplessness is involuntary.

We must break away from such wrong messages if we are to understand what rest really is. A graphic example of wrong programming occurred when a bright idea of Henry Ford's burned out. The infant automobile industry had just hailed his assembly-line concept as a history-making breakthrough. Ford, the great innovator, tried to compound his success by instituting a seven-day work week as well. Production soared as workers rose to the bait of more money. Then, gradually, accidents mounted, absenteeism multiplied, and worker discontent mushroomed. Upon investigation, Ford reluctantly conceded that people work better if they don't work all the time. In effect, Ford agreed with God, who long ago decreed, "Rest [a sabbath] is necessary."

Some Christians today could just as gracefully let go of the nineteenth-century dogma that keeping a day set apart for God should entail the effort of going to church three times on Sunday and feeling guilty about engaging in "worldly" activities, however innocent. Still ringing in our ears is literature which contains a depressing residue of stories about Victorian-age papas. Their sabbath rules, enforced without mercy or justice, were wearisome and tyrannical.

And yet, more relaxed Christians won't want to swing too far the other way on the pendulum of current national practice. Canceling out the Lord's Day in a welter of Sunday funnies, an endless litany chanted by sports announcers, and a weekend marathon of fun-seeking isn't the answer either.

Take the phenomenon of weekend roaming of the highways.

All who live in "Thither" seem seized by an urge to drive to "Yon," at the same time inhabitants of "Yon" drive obsessively to "Thither." If you have been part of this crowd, you may also have confused your inner clock with late Friday and Saturday nights and with sleeping in on Sunday morning. If so, you may be familiar with "Sunday-night insomnia," and you may know all too well why poor old Monday is tagged "blue."

Losing the meaning and purpose of the day of rest leads to loss of taste for little sabbaths—little rests. Rushing from one project to the next, complaining (bragging?) how busy we are, how exhausted, how in demand, we hide the real reason for our incessant hurrying. Secretly we theorize: A moving target is harder to hit, so if I keep going my enemies (whoever they may be) won't be able to get me. Those who think themselves pursued, you see, have no time to rest.

What might be a God-pleasing middle course?

First, if we stopped long enough to turn, face, and name our enemies, we could get off the not-so-merry-go-round. Then, viewing the day (or the night) at hand as worthwhile for its own sake, instead of forever mortgaging it for some future El Dorado, we could reclaim delight in dailyness. Also, foregoing our insatiable feeding on sensation, which is rooted in fear that we won't have time to live before some maniac blows us up, we could again savor each moment, each minor joy of living. Deliberately clearing our calendars, schedules, and appointment books could lead to a new humility, because we would see that the world does *not* collapse even though we are not, at that particular moment, holding it together. We could achieve the inner rest that is like being in the eye of the hurricane, where peace exists despite the fierce winds of adversity shaking the structure of life.

In our frenetic society, being at rest is not only rare, it is simply not understood. But deaf as the secular are, Christians who have the Bible to define *rest* for them are far more reprehensible if they refuse to hear that rest is more than cessation of activity, much more than mere sleep. Chiefly, the Scriptures say that Rest comes from the inner conviction that God is in control, precisely when events seem at their most uncontrollable. Generated from the spiritual realm and accepted in faith, this belief can affect physical/mental/emotional health as nothing else will.

If, for instance, we decide to believe that God allows, causes, or uses our insomnia for purposes not yet revealed and that we can trust His judgment more than our own we, by an act of will, learn the trusting "to be" and discard the obsessive "to do." What this can do for state of mind and its concomitant health must be experienced to be understood.

So try "resting in the Lord" vis-à-vis your insomnia. This basic exercise can condition you for more strenuous occasions such as preparing for major surgery, coping with an accident or a death, taking care of an invalid—or standing up for your faith in the face of threats. In short, you will be able to deal well with the crises we all must face. Learning how to rest in the Lord is like a fire drill. In all the years you attended elementary school, did your school ever burn down? Most of us say no, yet how familiar became the sudden ringing of the fire bell, how at ease we were, knowing it required our orderly marching out of the building to stand around giggling and shoving one another until harried teachers marched us back in again. (In isolated instances, when the building was on fire, lives were saved because children knew what to do and where to go.)

Conflagrations of life command our attention as abruptly as that fire bell. Unless we faithfully practice the drill we won't know how to find the shelter of peace from whatever wildfire ignites. You could begin now by devoting some of your wakeful time to studying Bible verses about rest. To help you, here are some examples from my own midnight journals, written while God was leading me from one understanding of rest to another.

First, I looked up *rest* and *resting* in my concordance,[1] then found the cited verses in the Amplified Bible. I began, where else, at the beginning. . . .

Genesis 2:2, 3:
And on the seventh day God ended His work. . . . And God
blessed (spoke good of) the seventh day, set it apart as His own . . .
because on it [He] rested from all His work. . . .

In my journal I wrote:

Surely God didn't rest on the seventh day because He was tired . . . was it to set us an example? When I finish some task, is this the kind of resting He wants me to do, too? He looked upon His work and said it was good . . . does He want me to stop and think about and look at my results, to see if all is as it should be?

Maybe resting in the satisfaction of a job well done is to give me a little taste of the joy of creation, a moment of refreshment, and a chance to thank Him for the privilege of work. Taking a break may also be valuable because it can keep me from charging headlong into the next project without consulting Him first.

The next reference took me into the Ten Commandments.

Exodus 20:8–10
[Earnestly] remember the sabbath day, to keep it holy [withdrawn
from common employment and dedicated to God] . . . the seventh

day is a sabbath to the Lord your God; in it you shall not do any work. . . .

My journal says:

What could God have had in mind, making rest on the seventh day one of His commandments? Didn't I read somewhere that in biblical times work never stopped for Gentiles except when the sun went down or they dropped dead from exhaustion?

Numbering the days in a seven-day cycle also was unheard of—only the occasional festival broke the monotony. Jews were considered unhinged because they refused to work on their holy day. No doubt, when they were slaves in Babylonia or living under Rome's heel, there were some bloody test cases when some of them died rather than disobey God. . . . A peculiar and stiff-necked people they may have been, but I admire their passionate belief in the Sabbath as their weekly reminder that "the Lord your God brought you out [of Egypt] with a mighty hand and an outstretched arm" (Deuteronomy 26:8).

But wandering in the labyrinth of history, Jews and Christians alike have lost the sense of celebration in the Sabbath. Alike, they have hung upon it chains of forbiddings, penalties, and punishments. Even today, hampered by obscure edicts pronounced centuries ago, conscientious Orthodox Jews scarcely dare move about on their Shabbat. It's a mystery how they can still regard it as "Queen of the Week" and a time of family closeness . . . where is Rest in this oppression of laws?

Christians can't judge them, though—the Law of Solemn Rest shows up in the New Testament, too . . . surely we shouldn't make inflexible what God intended as loving. How sad the Lord must be, to see what He intended as bonds of love forged into chains. Didn't Jesus say the Sabbath was made for (human)kind, not the other way around? How do *I* observe the Lord's Day of

Rest? Maybe I could try Frank Laubach's Game with Minutes,[2] which he borrowed from Brother Lawrence.[3]

Moment by moment throughout the day, I could silently ask Jesus, "Am I doing what You want me to do—now, this minute, Lord?"

A regular pause and check-in with Him could give me little rests whenever I'm off course. Then, at night, I could talk with Him about my day just past, asking Him to clear away rubbish I've strewn around—why not get right with God every night, not just on the Lord's Day? Yes, the relief of a nightly confession would clear the entrance into rest—maybe sleep, too. A conscience daily cleansed by God surely is the softest pillow, and closeness with Him the warmest cover . . . is that in the Bible?

Further exploration into rest uncovered a surprise.

Leviticus 25:4:
But in the seventh year there shall be a sabbath of solemn rest for the land . . . you shall neither sow your field, nor prune your vineyard.

In my journal I discussed this:

A Sabbath of rest for the land—for a whole year! And we think ecological awareness is so modern. It seems God created every living thing with an indwelling need for rest, but even so He allows the land to be at the mercy of man, who is often merciless in his greed for crops. The Dust Bowl of the 1930s showed us up as the worst kind of slave drivers, abusing the land. Come to think of it, we can be our own slave drivers, resisting the vital urge to rest, priding ourselves on burning out or wearing out "for the Lord." Wonder how God feels about this "favor" we do Him.

Wonder how, with a more humble spirit, we could use the wise farmer's adaptation of God's command to "let lie fallow."'

On another night an even more startling insight awaited.

Joshua 3:11, 13, 16, 17:
Behold, the ark of the covenant; the Lord of all the earth is passing over before you into Jordan!

When the soles of the feet of the priests who bear the ark of the Lord . . . shall rest in the Jordan, the waters of the Jordan coming down from above shall be cut off, and they shall stand in one heap.

Then the waters . . . stood and rose up in a heap far off . . . and the people passed over opposite Jericho . . . the priests . . . stood firm on dry ground in the midst of the Jordan, until all the nation finished passing over the Jordan.

My journal:

Thinking what these verses mean to me—it seems that resting my foot wherever God tells me to could bring about a miracle. I would settle for less—like some peace and harmony in this family of mine—but it makes me ponder . . . how often, without argument, have I put my foot where God directed? Or do I step where I choose and then complain when it turns out to be ankle-deep in mud—or worse? Strange, the connections you make. These words remind me of Psalms 119:105: "Your word is a lamp to my feet and a light to my path."

And this, in turn, reminds me of the days when movie theaters had ushers who led you down the dark aisles with a flashlight. In the blackness, you were utterly dependent on your usher . . . if I could trust an usher in a movie, why not trust You, Lord, in the same way?

More insights came. The unsavory story of David and Bathsheba contains many unexpected elements of rest, particularly in 1 Chronicles 22:9, but 1 Chronicles 28 made the most lasting impression.

1 Chronicles 28: 2, 3:
Then David the king . . . said . . . I myself intended to build a house of rest for the ark of the covenant. . . . But God said to me, You shall not . . . because you have been a man of war and have shed blood.

My journal records:

I see that God is no easy mark—He forgave David, but He also wouldn't let him build "a house of rest for the ark" because David had shed blood (specifically Uriah's). How evenhandedly God metes out mercy, love, and justice. Another side of this—a "house of rest for the ark"—can be taken to mean that as a believer I should prepare a resting place within myself fit for the Shekinah, the Glory Presence. Then I would never know an absence of rest—the indwelling Presence of God is my Rest . . . Lord, only You can make me fit to be Your house. . . .

Coming to rest in the Psalms after this felt like drifting into quiet backwaters after a wild ride down the Clackamas River in a leaky rubber raft.

Psalms 16:7–9:
I will bless the Lord Who has given me counsel; yes, my heart instructs me in the night seasons. . . . my glory [my inner self] rejoices; my body too shall rest and confidently dwell in safety.

My journal response:

What promises of gladness these instructions sent in the night bring! Now, Lord, if only I will follow Your guidance.

Another psalm spoke so strongly I underlined bits in red. Previously, I had written a date in my Bible to mark the time in April 1969 when my ears were opened to God by the Poet/King who declares:

Psalms 37: 1, 3, 4, 5, 7, 8:
   Fret not yourself because of evildoers. . . .
   Trust . . . in the Lord, and do good. . . . Delight yourself also in the Lord. . . . Commit your way to the Lord . . . repose [each care of] your road on Him. . . .
   Be still and rest in the Lord. . . . Cease from anger and forsake wrath. . . .

My journal:

This entire psalm, Father, gives me fresh hope after having survived a very difficult day. Tomorrow looks like it will be hard, too, but right now I feel as though I've received a recharge of spiritual oxygen. I think I can get some rest after all—maybe sleep a little . . . but it doesn't matter, if I sleep or not, that is, because I know You are here. Thank You—and good night.

Another night—but this time I feel so like a fox pursued by dogs I could gladly dig a hole and pull it in after me. All too well I understand what fox hunters mean when they say "gone to earth." Huddled in bed, covers pulled high, I feel warm but not safe from the hounds of trouble snuffling around my hideaway. Even harder is to leave my sleepless bed, get my Bible, and look for comfort—at 2:00 A.M. it all seems pointless . . . but I will try Psalm 37 again. . . .

Then I found a kindred soul in another fugitive. *Psalm 55*—all twenty-three verses—showed me how to cry out boldly for help. The Psalmist plunges right in, demanding God's attention, not bothering with so much as a "please" or a "dear Father."

"Listen," he commands, "hide not Yourself. . . !" "Attend to me, and answer me. . . ." His peremptory shout to God takes my breath away. Then David lays out every doubt, fear, and pain before his sovereign Lord. You can almost see him pacing the floor, wringing his hands. He teaches me there are times when courtesy and reverence do not get top priority.

Verses 2–5:
I am restless and distraught . . . [I] must moan; [I am distracted] by the noise of the enemy . . . the oppression and threatenings. . . . My heart is grievously pained . . . the terrors of death have fallen upon me. Fear and trembling are come upon me; horror and fright have overwhelmed me.

My Journal:

It is so comforting to learn that David sometimes wanted to bail out, too. He longs, absurdly, for the wings of a dove so he can fly away and be at rest. How he rants, on and on for fifteen verses, pleading with God, talking to himself, sometimes talking to his absent friend/turncoat.

Then, after all this Sturm und Drang, David calms down and becomes reflective. Getting rid of all his pent-up feelings apparently cleared space for cooler thinking and the beginnings of healing. His next words speak deeply to me: "As for me, I will call upon God; and the Lord will save me" (verse 16).

He reminds himself of all the good God has done for him in the past. Finally, in verse 22 (is he talking to himself or to me?) he urges, "Cast your burden on the Lord [releasing the weight of it] and He will sustain you. . . ." But in spite of this calmer, softer mood, David can't resist hinting to God how He should deal with David's enemies.

Verse 23:
But You, O God, will bring down the wicked to the pit of destruction; men of blood and treachery shall not live out half their days; but I will trust, lean on and confidently rely on You.

My journal:

How alike David and I are. I see myself in his frank desire to escape his problems, in his relish and thirst for revenge, and in his recollecting himself in time to remember he shouldn't be telling God how to "get even." We are alike, too, in the comfort we get from putting our feelings into words—I'm quickly learning the value of this scratching away in my midnight journal.

One more psalm stands out.

Psalms 94:18, 19:
When I said, My foot is slipping, Your mercy and loving-kindness, O Lord, held me up. In the multitude of my (anxious) thoughts within me, Your comforts cheer and delight my soul!

My journal:

How I love the part about the slipping foot . . . if You could hold King David steady, Lord, could You do the same for me? Father, the ground seems very unsteady right now . . . I claim David's affirmation for my own.

Moving on to Isaiah, I found a secret God had hidden there for me to find.

Isaiah 28:12:
The Lord had said, This is the true rest [the way to true comfort and happiness] that you shall give to the weary, and this is the true refreshing.

My journal:

Lord, You have revealed the secret in Your Word—the Book, which reveals the Word—Your Son. When You say, "Enter into My Rest," I hear You telling me to "believe Jesus." It's so simple—why couldn't I see it before? Is that why You've been keeping me awake—trying to get through to me for this?

Deeper into Isaiah came more assurance.

Isaiah 30:15:
For thus said the Lord God, the Holy One of Israel, In returning to Me and resting in Me you shall be saved; in quietness and in (trusting) confidence shall be your strength.

My journal:

This fills me with peace, but the next short sentence touches me the most, Father: "And you would not . . . you said, No!"
Verses 16 and 17 describe so perfectly the cause and effect of running aimlessly about, defying You and speeding on "our own course" like a drunken driver. If it weren't so sad it would be funny.

Then comes that poignant eighteenth verse: "And therefore the Lord [earnestly] waits—expectant, looking and longing—to be gracious to you. . . ."

The picture I have of You, my waiting Father, longing to be gracious to me, however heedless and selfish I may be, starts tears in my eyes.

Next, a new direction turned out to be an old one, rediscovered by the heart:

Jeremiah 6:16 and Matthew 11:28, 29:
Thus says the Lord, Stand by the roads and look, and ask for the eternal paths, where is the good, old way; then walk in it, and you will find rest. . . .

Come to Me, all you who labor and are heavy-laden . . . and I will cause you to rest—I will ease and relieve and refresh your souls. Take My yoke upon you, and learn of Me . . . you will find rest—relief, ease and refreshment and recreation and blessed quiet. . . .

My journal:

Why am I so surprised that both Testaments reveal You to be the same God? They sing in harmony about "the good old way." If I find no rest, Lord, it must be because I balk at Your invitation to walk on it. Now I hear You, Jesus, clearly say, "I Am the Way" and I know I will reach my longed-for destination—Rest—as soon as I study the road map in Your Book.

Other truths, hidden to be found, like Easter eggs for the children, awaited my next exploration.

What *Is* Rest, Really?

2 Corinthians 12:8, 9:
Three times I called upon the Lord and . . . begged that [the thorn
in my flesh] *might depart from me; But He said to me, My grace
. . . [is] enough for you . . . for My strength and power are made
perfect—fulfilled and completed and show themselves most
effective—in [your] weakness. Therefore, I will all the more gladly
glory in my weaknesses and infirmities, that the strength and
power of Christ . . . may rest—yes, may pitch a tent [over] and
dwell—upon me!*

My journal:

Lord, I see that the more I admit my weaknesses, the more Your
spirit covers me like a tent, giving shade, rest, and refuge. I feel
a little dizzy, realizing that as soon as I admit my inadequacies I
am released from trying to hide them. How much energy I've
wasted masquerading as strong because I thought I must.

The last reading seems a large chunk, but so was my hunger
for help.

Hebrews Chapters 3 and 4:
One verse from this selection sums up what reading the Bible has
come to mean to me—I can't adequately express the sense of
inner rest it brings.

Hebrews 4:12:
*For the Word that God speaks is alive and full of power—making
it active, operative, energizing and effective; it is sharper than any
two-edged sword, penetrating to the dividing line of the breath of
life . . . and . . . spirit, and of joints and marrow [that is, of the
deepest parts of our nature] exposing and sifting and analyzing
and judging the very thoughts and purposes of the heart.*

My journal response:

Father, right this minute I feel I am being pierced by the scalpel of Your Word. At the same time it hurts, it heals. These two chapters assure me I am among those You love.

Thank You—my feelings go far beyond anything I can write . . . thank You for waking me up sometimes, for keeping me awake other times, for gently dinging away at me until I finally got up and opened my Bible. I want to live from now on in the light of this new knowledge of Your love—it touches both head and heart.

Today, as I think about my midnight encounters with God, the sensation I associate with the infilling of His Holy Spirit sweeps over me like a sudden, pleasant chill. A mental acuity beyond intellect gives me an ability to read between the lines of the Bible.

There, shining between the words that lie on the pages in orderly ranks, is still another intimate word for me from my Father. This ability is not exclusive but is given to anyone who by obedience opens his/her spirit to God. Through His Book He speaks, and His Word is more alive than we are.

The Bible is a magnifying glass, putting into sharp focus what really matters in life. That is this: to forget self and fear and the unruly mob of hobgoblins called the "what ifs" that will move in if allowed house room; to look instead at the truth our myopic souls miss. God is far bigger than anything we can imagine.

The Bible magnifies God to help our spiritually weak eyes see Him, to comprehend His bigness. Thus, the more you let the Bible speak to you, the more you rivet your attention on God, the more He will help you learn how to help yourself, awake or asleep.

Yes, even while you sleep. Modern sleep researchers are now satisfied that the mind never shuts down completely but continues to work on whatever you were concerned with while awake. Actually, your unconscious works better when you are asleep because you are not bombarding it with conflicting messages. To feed your unconscious nourishing food on which to chew while you sleep, try filling your mind with verses like those I shared. Someone has said that the last thought you think before going to sleep will be your first thought upon awakening in the morning, possibly because your unfettered unconscious worked on it all night.

So, when you return to bed after studying your Bible, tell your unconscious to incorporate all you've learned into your memory bank. The part of your self named *Junior* by Agnes Sanford[4] and defined as "your unconscious experience"[5] will obey you. In a rich mingle, your busy brain will blend your intuitive, creative nature (often suppressed in consciousness) with your cognitive, logical self to give back to you thoughts you didn't know you could think.

As you pull the covers up, say something like this:

Junior, I want you to work on these verses I read tonight. I know that once they entered my brain through my eyes they were mine forever. Be ready with feedback in the morning.

Putting yourself into God's safe care (never go to bed without it), relax, rest in the assurance that you are on the way—God's way—to wholeness. You might mull over a phrase, a verse (a single word will do) that gives you a sense of rest to recall it. Then, if you wish, think of God's arms surrounding you like the warmth of a comforter, yes, the Comforter who is indispensable to Rest. We all need comfort—or do we?

References and Suggested Midnight Reading

1. In the fifty-eight places *rest* is cited in *The Bible Reader's Encyclopedia and Concordance*, some refer to it as "remainder"; of those which refer to repose, refuge, ease, and tranquillity, these samples are only a choice few.

2. Frank C. Laubach, *Christ Liveth in Me* and *Game With Minutes* (Old Tappan, New Jersey: Fleming H. Revell Company, 1961).

3. Brother Lawrence, *Practice of the Presence of God* (Old Tappan, New Jersey: Fleming H. Revell Company, 1958).

4. Agnes Sanford, *The Healing Light*, revised edition (Saint Paul, Minnesota: Macalester Park Publishing Company, 1972).

5. Rollo May, *Courage to Create* (New York: W.W. Norton & Co., Inc., 1975), pp. 51, 52.

Six ★
The
Comforter

"Not everybody needs comfort," some would say. An evangelist once advised, "Don't waste time trying to convert someone who thinks he doesn't need Jesus any more than you would try to give a blanket to someone who isn't cold."

· Good advice. The man working at a job he enjoys, who is happy with family or spouse, is in good health, who can smile as he mentally counts his hidden cache of Krügerrands, who has just received a hefty rebate on his new car, feels no need for the Savior—or a Comforter.

Only when a man feels the bottom of the pit pressing against his back, only when a doctor's prognosis scatters hope like houses in a hurricane, only when grief or shame or pain destroys all illusions of security, is he ready to appeal to God for comfort and help. Even then he may not see God as Comforter, as anxious thoughts crowd his mind:

> I can't go crawling to God now, when I never took much notice of Him before. . . . Better not call God's attention to me—I've done some things. . . . Why has God got it in for me? I'm no worse than anybody else. . . .

Scared and defensive though he may be, that man is now ready for news as comforting as a negative biopsy report. His ears are open to hear Jesus say, "Come to Me . . . I will ease your soul."

Ready to give His Good News directly or by ways as subtle, varied, and complicated as the humans who are in distress, God tailors comfort to individual needs. For the insomniac, He may use or even cause sleeplessness for purposes far beyond our ken—as uncomforting a thought as ever was.

Why do we get so upset at the thought of God interrupting or preventing sleep? Do we secretly fear that He actually is a wrathful God bent on punishing us? Do we think withholding sleep is a whip He holds over us? Accepting wakefulness, instead, as a signal from God to seek closer accord with Him can bring a new peaceful inner awareness of Him as Comforter.

For instance, Catherine Marshall describes how chronic illness drove her to pray the Prayer of Relinquishment. That surrender went like this:

> "I'm tired of asking" was the burden of my prayer.
>   I'm beaten, finished. God, You decide what You want for me for the rest of my life.[1]

Surrender changed her from a rebel to a person who carried an unquenchable glow of comfort to thousands. That same unqualified conceding to God can unlock the prison of insomnia, too.

This means that although sleep may stay away again tonight, if we relinquish our wakefulness to God He can comfort, heal, and then give us a new beginning—a good trade for mere sleep.

For those whose chronic physical condition or medical problem makes sleeping difficult, this advice might seem simplistic—and it would be wrong to imply that such a nighttime pact with God guarantees instant physical healing. What is guaranteed is that the healing process activated in your mind and emotions by this relinquishment will improve your body's homeopathic ability to mend and heal itself.[2]

There is no way your mind, if it is churning with bitterness and fear, can bring comfort to your sick body. Coauthors Phillip Goldberg and Daniel Kaufman state, "Insomnia is not a disease . . . it is a sign . . . a complaint that chronic insomniacs are somehow out of whack with the rhythms nature implanted in us."[3] Later, they add, "Only recently have we [begun again] treating the whole person . . . in ancient traditional cultures the healing arts tended to view symptoms as . . . malfunctions involving the body as a whole."[4]

Substitute "God" for "nature" in their first statement and you hear the Creator/Physician offering healing that is harmonious with His original scenario for humankind. That kind of comfort cannot be topped.

Consider the victim of sleep apnea, who may awaken as many as five hundred times during the night because he is unable to sleep and breathe at the same time. For him, there is no comfort anywhere, certainly not in bed. But sleep experts can now diagnose and treat this dysfunction successfully with "various drugs and by a simple surgical procedure. . . ."[5]

Not taking anything away from this scientific breakthrough, we should realize that another barrier (psychic), erected as a result of countless nights of fighting to breathe (and the subsequent lack of deep sleep), still stands untouched. This barrier must be breached by something more powerful than medication and "a small valve inserted in the trachea."[6]

Every night, the specter of anxiety and apprehension gets into bed with the apnea victim, causing adrenaline to pump through his body and kill sleep. Because to sleep means to involuntarily flirt with death, there is no comfort in Shakespeare's praise of sleep "that knits up the ravell'd sleave of care. . . ."[7]

Instead, the apneac person may be so confused he feeds his mind mixed instructions on how to deal with this stress. At the same time he goes to bed ready to fight—for his will to live is powerful—he prepares for the night wondering if living is worth this nightly combat.

Hans Selye, the Canadian stress research pioneer, whose phrase "fight or flight" became part of the lexicon of the literature on stress, would agree. He taught us that we react to stress by ignoring or adapting, by fighting or running away.[8] Sometimes, like the man with apnea, we try to do them all at the same time.

In his confusion, the apneac's protests of "Why me?" and "What have I done to deserve this?" erode deep into his being, triggering the inevitable search for someone or something to blame. At that moment, the Prayer of Relinquishment and its accompanying comfort is crucial to healing. God is the only Physician who can heal him—body/mind/spirit. Even the insertion of a trachea valve which will restore his ability to breathe and sleep at the same time will not wipe away the conviction that he has been unfairly treated, because spiritual unrest resists all the ministrations of medical science. He is as defeated and comfortless as the prisoner who, having given up all hope of escape, tries to make a pillow of his chains.

Another example—a woman had a nagging pain in her abdomen but insisted it was nothing although she was surreptitiously dosing herself with painkillers. Haunted by fear of cancer, she struggled through sleepless nights when dull pain gnawed monotonously. The mounting panic she tried to deny finally climaxed one night when the nuisance of pain exploded into an agony of pain.

Rushed to the hospital, her problem was diagnosed. Cancer? No, hot appendix. Next stop—the operating room. In spite of her self-diagnosis and unfounded fear of the wrong problem, she survived a possible fatal peritonitis.

At home one day during her recuperation, the woman walked out on the patio, took a deep breath of the warm summer air, and stretched—carefully. Smiling at her husband, she exclaimed, "God—it's good to be alive!" Then she added, "I guess that was a prayer of thanksgiving."

We could say she was "lucky," but what is luck except one of God's nicknames? She had learned to value the gift of life—and the Giver.

Insomniacs could learn something from that woman, so graciously given back her life. We, too, sometimes stubbornly refuse to take our hurts to the Great Physician, wanting comfort but fearing His diagnosis. Even as the creeping sepsis of fear poisons our lives, causing ever-increasing spiritual pain, we try to doctor ourselves, a cold comfort indeed.

To freely admit "we have sinned"[9] and to confess those sins is like the woman's trip to the emergency room—we go only if pushed by circumstances. To ask God to "(dismiss our lawlessness) and continuously cleanse us from . . . everything not in conformity to His will"[10] is to submit to the comfort of His healing knife of forgiveness that cuts away the disease of sin. Then, healed, we can add our cry: "God—it's good to be alive!"

Whether you struggle nightly with apnea or find life full of stresses you can't handle during the day so you fight with them all night—whatever your condition, God waits to comfort you. If you accept the idea that healing begins within, in your mind and emotions, by His cleansing grace God will set your own homeopathic powers in motion. That may have been Jesus' intent when He promised us the Comforter.

When Jesus told the disciples that if He didn't go away the Comforter could not come, He was telling us, too, that this mysterious God, likened in the Bible to both Father and Mother, and compared to a refuge, a fortress, a "mighty Rock in a weary land"—this God is our "safe house." The more we let Him into our lives the more He shows us He is "for" us.

If you have ever imaged the protective arm of God around you so vividly that you could feel His warmth, you might also relate that to a certain cold night sometime in your life when you went to bed hoping that tonight, for a change, you would be able to sleep, but not feeling very optimistic. Pulling the covers up snugly around your ears to shut out the world, you created a cocoon of comfort for yourself.

Maybe that coverlet was a handmade quilt, maybe a gift from Grandma. A store-bought quilt could keep you just as warm, but there was something special about that lovingly hand-stitched-

and-tied comforter that made you feel good. When you thought "comforter" you meant Grandma as much as her gift. Remember clinging to her hand when you were little? Even now you can feel how warm and strong it felt, and how her eyes twinkled when you entrusted some childish dream to her. As for fun—she could always think of ways to have fun although there was little money. It was so like Grandma and her habit of "making do"—in the same way she could fashion leftover scraps into a quilt top in the Star of Bethlehem or Wedding Ring pattern. Her caring industry said good things about the comforting continuity of family.

For you, her gift of a quilt was more than a cover for a cold night; it was a link with all you value. Receiving it from her hands, you resolved to take such good care of it that someday *your* grandchildren would receive it and cherish it just as you do. Curling up, now, to sleep under Grandma's quilt, the warmth and weight of something more than cloth comforts you. The sense of belonging, something every human being holds dear, makes you feel safe.

The spiritual counterpart of Grandma's gift is God's Comforter. We're not talking exclusively about the Third Person of the Trinity this time, although *Comforter* is one of His names. Here, the Comforter is a covering God has made in His Faithfulness pattern to give to every believer. Better than any comforter made by human hands, His Comforter is the unshakable conviction that He loves us. We need never huddle shivering and abandoned through any dark night of the soul where, as F. Scott Fitzgerald said, out of his own sad experience, ". . . it's always three o'clock in the morning."[11]

Think how lavishly God covers us. Prudent Grandma saved worn-out shirts and dresses, piecing the best parts together to make a quilt top, but God uses only the ever-new seamless fabric of His trustworthiness. Imagine, with me, God's Quilt as He might describe it:

First, I outline the master design
in My most beautiful blues—from a
summer sky, from the peacock's feather,
from a laughing baby's eye.
Seeing the blue, man and woman will remember
that they can rest on My promises always.

I scatter sparkles of rainbow throughout,
those flashing hues of joy, and then I add
the stark black stitchery of My own pain
suffered when My Son died on the Cross.

The red, red blossoms of His blood bloom
on that Tree, circled in the purity white
of His sinlessness, a garden where My other
children know they are safe.

Green, the green of returning spring, speaks
of His eternalness.

For borders, I use the limits of man's own finite mind and,
in pity because I love My children,
I do not ask them to venture beyond into
the Cold, the Cold where only Infinite
can breathe and think.

See how intricately My plans weave in and out . . .
like iridescent silken skeins they change and
interchange.
See how the golden cord of My will shines
more gloriously whenever the silver thread
of human will intertwines in obedience to Mine.

I make the Comforter long enough and wide enough
to cover them in every crisis. I make it strong,
so strong not even the cruelest wind of, hate,

not even the dead-cold hand of the Adversary
can rip it away.

To finish, My filling is My Holy Spirit, perfect
Insulator against the endless cold of separation
that shrivels the souls of those who reject Me.

To all who long for the encircling warmth of My love,
I freely give My Comforter.

As you draw this divine quilt up around your shivering spirit, savoring the warmth that envelops you, know that this coverlet will shelter you no matter what icy wind blows. God's Quilt is soft and warm, yet as tough as tempered steel. Ordinary covers will tear and eventually wear thin, but His coverlet, fashioned in the Faithfulness pattern, will never need repair.

If this sounds like a "security blanket," so be it. Our great need is to admit that we cannot survive without one. When Charles Schulz invented Linus and his blanket, he did his readers a favor, although we've all laughed at Schulz' little joke, taking this character to symbolize anyone who seems insecure. How superior we've felt, to see Linus clutching his blanket or having an anxiety attack whenever it was taken from him to be washed. There he would sit, staring at the washing machine, or pacing the floor while his blanket tumbled, forever it seemed, in the dryer. As time inched by, the circles under his eyes grew bigger and blacker. But Linus knew where his security lay. He was not too proud to admit that he wouldn't be happy until his beloved blanket was once again tucked up against his left ear, his thumb securely in his mouth.

Linus' blanket becomes doubly significant when we see that it doubles as a weapon. Linus could "zap" his enemies with the "fastest blanket in the west" before they knew what hit them. Whatever parallel we draw from that for ourselves, we realize that to Linus his blanket represents comfort—and omnipotence.

Unlikely though it seems, Schulz is echoing Paul. In 2 Corinthians 1, Paul repeats "comfort" in an extraordinary manner. Verses 3 and 4 demonstrate:

> Blessed [be] the God and Father of our Lord Jesus Christ, the Father of sympathy (pity and mercies) and the God [Who is the Source] of every consolation and **comfort** and encouragement; Who consoles and **comforts** and encourages us in every trouble (calamity and affliction), so that we may also be able to console (**comfort** and encourage) those who are in any kind of trouble or distress, with the consolation (**comfort** and encouragement) with which we ourselves are consoled and **comforted** and encouraged by God (emphasis added).

Paul may have been recalling the prophetic words of Isaiah's fortieth chapter, where God's comfort is extended to His disobedient children, the Israelites, after they had been chastised. If you are a student in God's night school, beginning to learn about obedience, you could forget to worry about your insomnia as these majestic verses (1, 2) fill your thoughts:

> Comfort, comfort My people, says your God. Speak tenderly to the heart of Jerusalem and cry to her that . . . her warfare [is] ended . . . her iniquity is pardoned.

These words beckon like a light in the forest on a stormy night, showing the way to refuge, a place by the fire for the lost traveler. There, chilled body and spirit can get warm again. Life is strangely like that stormy night, noisy with nature's threats. Sleep, blown away on the importunate wind of worry, seems something you barely remember from childhood. With longing, you recall how easily your head dropped to the welcoming pillow as your mother kissed you and whispered, "May God watch over you—sleep well," and tucked the coverlet around you.

Secure in her love, you slept. But for those who have no such happy memory, is there no hope? Yes, there is, for God is like the best mother you could imagine. He yearns to give you comfort and shelter the same way He gave it to His beloved Israel. In the last chapter of Isaiah (66:13), foretelling the restoration of Israel as a nation "born in a day" (a prophecy fulfilled in 1948), God says, "As one whom his mother comforts, so will I comfort you; you shall be comforted in Jerusalem."

Tonight, when you go to bed, let God tuck His Comforter around you. As His love touches you, soft as a mother's kiss, you may hear Him whisper, "I will watch over you—sleep well."

You see, it's safe to believe this, because God never sleeps; He doesn't need sleep. So if you can trust God to be on guard, all your night fears no longer will have power over you. For the person victimized by "insomniac's paradox," the way to get rid of the sleeplessness that rises out of fear of going to sleep is at hand.

References and Suggested Midnight Reading

1. Catherine Marshall, *Beyond Ourselves* (New York: McGraw-Hill Book Company, 1961).

2. Hans Selye, *Stress Without Distress* (New York: Harper & Row Publishers, Inc., 1974).

3. Phillip Goldberg and Daniel Kaufman, *Natural Sleep: How to*

Get Your Share (Emmaus, Pennsylvania: Rodale Printing, Inc., 1978).

4. Ibid.

5. Alice K. Schwartz and Norma S. Aaron, *Somniquest: The Five Types of Sleeplessness and How to Overcome Them* (New York: Harmony Books, 1979).

6. Ibid.

7. William Shakespeare, *Macbeth*, Act II, scene 2.

8. Selye, *Stress Without Distress*.

9. First John 1:9 AMPLIFIED.

10. Ibid.

11. F. Scott Fitzgerald, *The Crack-Up* (New York: New Directions Books, 1956), p. 75.

. . . in a real dark night of the soul it is always three o'clock in the morning. . . .

Seven ★ _____
God Is Awake,
so It's
Safe to Sleep

Insomniacs' paradox begins with "What if," a question insomniacs ask staring into the dark, seldom with optimism. Sleepless, we fear sleep itself, wondering, "What if I *do* go to sleep—I have a little control over my life when I'm awake, but asleep I have *no* control . . . what if . . .

>   a burglar or a rapist breaks in . . .
>   a heart attack sneaks up on me . . .
>   the house catches on fire . . .
>   some maniac pushes The Button . . .
>   someone I love dies suddenly . . .
>   I have terrible dreams foretelling catastrophe . . .
>   the Lord returns, and I'm not ready . . .

tomorrow comes and it's worse than today . . .
sleep really is like dying, and I'm afraid to die.

At the same time, we know (or think we know) that we *must get to sleep*. From childhood on, we've heard:

(Mother say) "If you don't get your sleep you'll be sick."
   (Benjamin Franklin say) "Early to bed and early to rise makes a man healthy, wealthy, and wise."
   (Ourselves say) "I must get to sleep so I can do my job."
   (Medical research say) "You want to know how important sleep is? Look at the millions of dollars and expert scientist-hours we're pouring into getting you back to sleep."
   (Our doctors say) "Having trouble sleeping? I'd better give you some pills."

On and on goes the counsel of fear, impressing on us in ways both subtle and crass, "You must sleep—or else."

Caught in a double bind, like a spider at the bottom of a bathtub, you feel hopeless. But there *is* hope. Some therapists now use the double bind to help their patients confront problems instead of evading them, teaching them not to resign themselves to an unacceptable either-or. In the case of insomnia, this means not settling for "either I get sick from not sleeping or I get hooked on pills that knock me out."

An alternative to the counsel of fear includes five points:

First, refuse to allow your mind to scare you with "what ifs." Brooding on events that haven't happened and probably never will can infect your imagination until feverish assumptions block out rational thinking.

Second, take this quote as an echo of God's wisdom: "Wakefulness in time of stress is an adaptive survival mechanism and the mark of a healthy person."[1]

You have been given permission to be awake at night from both God and man, so now grant yourself permission. Healthy solutions to your stress are knocking at your bedroom door. Although you cannot change the world by sleeping any more than you can change it by not sleeping, being willing to revise your attitude toward events and conditions is a better way to gain peace. It's time to heed the truism, "If what you are doing doesn't work, try something else."

Third, deal with your fear realistically. Whether you are afraid to go to sleep or are afraid because you can't sleep, you needn't be ashamed of your fear. Feel afraid and admit it. This does not mean you are inadequate as a human being or as a Christian but is an exhibition of normal anxiety symptoms. One doctor assures us:

> Fear is an illness . . . not transmitted by germs or by viruses . . . [it] flourishes in epidemic form in this harassed twentieth century. A frank expression of anxiety to a doctor or religious counselor can open new horizons . . . for emancipation from fear.[2]

Fourth, don't take yourself so seriously. This is not to say that "sleeper's fear of the bed, a psychic anxiety"[3] is not real, or that "agrypnia-phobia" (fear of sleeplessness)[4] is not an actual, difficult condition. It's just so much better to turn your sense of humor loose. Not only is laughing at yourself a benevolent addiction, it's easy on the budget.

Keeping a scrapbook of humor and philosophical sayings about insomnia, recommended earlier,[5] can help you cultivate a light touch. Most insomniacs are so *solemn* about their sleeping difficulties. Only the few who can laugh about their wakefulness are conquering their erstwhile enemy of the night. They have learned, as one wag puts it, "Insomnia is much ado about nodding."[6]

Laughter, or "a merry heart," as Proverbs 17:22 tells us, "doeth good like a medicine" (kjv).

One of the best contemporary evidences of laughter power is found in Norman Cousins' *Anatomy of an Illness.* His problem, far worse than insomnia, had been diagnosed as an incurable collagen disease. Desperately ill, in pain most of the time despite heavy medication, he decided to take radical action. Insomniacs should do themselves a favor by reading his story about watching old Marx Brothers and Laurel and Hardy movies.[7]

He recalls, "Ten minutes of belly laughter gave me two hours of pain-free sleep."[8] His whoops of laughter so disturbed other patients in the hospital that he finally moved to a hotel where, he relates, the service was better, the surroundings quieter and more private, and nobody cared if he laughed.

He describes how laughter caused a cumulative drop in sedimentation rate in his blood, a significant event in his particular illness.

Cousins' doctor, who deserves recognition as a pioneer in doctor/patient relationships, became so fascinated by Cousins' quixotic refusal to give up and die that he made his patient a partner in his own treatment, thereby strengthening Cousins' will to live. At the same time, their team approach to medicine provided an apt example of our society's growing "holism" movement, defined in Cousins' book as "the movement from awareness of disease to knowledge of human beings in whom disease exists."[9]

If laughter therapy worked for Cousins, it can work for the insomniac. A typical poor sleeper, described in the literature on insomnia as "repressive, with lack of ability to express basic drives," says, "When you don't sleep well you suffer."[10]

He sees himself as "staring into the dark as though chained to the bed." He feels "hopeless, tormented, disembodied, lonely, thinking of himself as a corpse."[11]

As a liberated insomniac, I sympathize—to a point. But then I want to laugh and chide, "Oh, come on . . . don't you see the joke of lying there in bed scaring yourself?"

The fifth point is best made through the following true stories about three people who dealt with their fear of sleeping, and how their solutions affected their lives. Some names have been changed, but all incidents are documented.

Betty's Story

One September, when my husband and I were enjoying a brief holiday at Gold Beach on the Oregon coast, we rented a small motel unit where I could write while he fished the Rogue River, which runs into the ocean at that location.

The maid, Betty, came in one morning to clean while I was busy typing. When she asked what I was writing and I replied, "A book about insomnia," she needed no prompting to volunteer her own encounter with sleeplessness and terror.

When she was seventeen, Betty lived with her mother, Mary, and her stepfather, Dan. One evening an old friend of Mary

105

came to town and, as Mary tried to convince Dan, wanted her to go out and have a cup of coffee with him just to talk over old times. But, Betty recalls, "Dan was blind jealous."

The same evening, Betty came home late from a date. She says she has always thanked the Lord she came home first.

The house was completely dark, not an unusual occurrence. As Betty turned the doorknob to come inside, her attention was distracted by having to lift the door a bit—it had a tendency to stick. Just as she stepped across the threshold she heard the thud and rush of heavy feet. A flood of curses polluted the air and a man's form loomed over her. When she saw the gleam of a butcher knife in his fist, she screamed, "No—don't!"

Shocked, Betty's stepfather skidded to a halt, the knife quivering an inch or two from her body. Then, slumping to the floor in an alcoholic stupor, Dan muttered, "I thought you was Mary—I thought you was Mary . . . Mary, I'll getcha fer goin' out with that guy. . . ."

Later that night Dan became so violent Betty's mother called the police, who had to take him away under restraint. But after a short stay in the prison hospital, he was released to come back home and confront two terrified women. A three-month reign of fear ensued, of never knowing when he might go berserk again. Somehow, then, Mary forced Dan to leave. Several years later, Betty adds, Dan had himself committed to a hospital for psychiatric care.

During those three nightmare months while Dan roamed the house like a wild animal on the loose, Betty says, "I never slept at all—well, no more than an hour or two any night. I was afraid of him and of what he might do to me or to Mom."

How could Betty, or Mary, hang on to sanity while living with a potential murderer? Whether or not Dan meant to kill Mary, if

Betty hadn't screamed or if her mother had come home first, one of them could have been dead. Mulling over such terrifying thoughts, it's not surprising that Betty, in spite of sleeping pills, couldn't sleep, or that Mary would tiptoe into Betty's room at odd hours of the night to make sure she was all right.

"Do you think you were trusting God through all this?"

"Well—yes, I trusted God. But I sure didn't trust Dan!"

Now in her thirties, Betty says that once Dan was out of the house for good, her insomnia ceased.

Clearly, Betty reacted to danger by instructing her midbrain to stay awake and on guard as long as she felt threatened, even though she was unaware of doing so. You could say her insomnia was the result of her "awake" switch being tied down in the "on" position. Young in faith as well as in years, Betty didn't know how to let God protect her, so He used her RAS (Reticular Activating System),[12] working from her unconscious to keep her awake, safe, and sane. More will be said about this in chapter 8.

No one can fault teenage Betty for not being able to trust God so totally she would be able to sleep no matter who threatened her life. Much ongoing experience with God, who patiently waits out our trusting/not trusting/trusting Him again, must occur before we are able to lie down in the midst of danger and "rest in the Lord." How this gives a person the weapons needed to combat fear is told in the next story, which strangely enough began in a home where toying with the occult was the norm.

Elsie's Story

Elsie grew up in a comfortable, happy home, the seventh child of free-thinker parents who didn't attend church but did allow their children to go to Sunday school. At the same time Elsie was being exposed to the Gospel, her father, an insatiable dabbler into the arcane and its arts, was becoming adept at casting horoscopes, even to making a chart for Elsie. He also introduced her to the pendulum, a device which works on the same principle as the Ouija board. Her mother, a second-generation Christian Scientist, lived strictly by that sect's doctrines, which deny the reality of sin and pain.

Elsie says, "I thought maybe there was a God . . . but then again maybe He was something parents made up to get kids to mind. People talk about the 'faith of a child' but I was a very critical, doubting child. Over and over, my Sunday-school teacher told me I needed to feel guilty and repent to be saved. I didn't feel I needed a Savior."

When she was fourteen, Elsie dreamed it was Judgment Day and that a face, its eyes closed, was coming toward her through clouds where

> . . . sunbeams, as suddenly as though turning to ice, became great arches of solid white. Through the arches you could see blue sky . . . and this Face, getting bigger and bigger.
>
> Then the Face stopped, right up against my open window . . . and I knew it was going to open its eyes and look at me . . . I'm glad I never dreamed of that Face with its eyes open . . . I was so scared—I knew at that moment how much I needed a Savior.
>
> Years of being afraid of God, whose Face I'd seen in my dream and accepted as real, passed before I literally fell in love with Jesus while studying His Sermon on the Mount. Later, I learned to love God as my Father, too, but Jesus was easier to picture and to believe loved me.

When in her middle thirties and a professing Christian, Elsie admits she still couldn't resist "fiddling with the pendulum." She also tells about becoming entranced with reincarnation.

"One night I prayed, 'If I ever lived before, would you please show me?' "

In an instant, she found herself astride a horse.

In front of me, just disappearing into a screen of brush, rode two men in chain mail, wearing red sashes. I could draw a picture of how they looked, on horseback, trotting along in front of me. Then the green bushes swished shut behind the men, blocking them from my sight. I recall no sense of asking to come back—but I woke myself up or came back from wherever I'd gone, trembling with fear.

I know the vision, or whatever it was, had been sent by Satan, not God. Maybe my asking, my prying into reincarnation, made me vulnerable. . . .

Years later Elsie's father died, having become a Christian just in time. Elsie's mother, suffering from Parkinson's Disease and crippling arthritis, began hallucinating that he was back, lying in bed beside her. Even though she stopped taking the drugs her doctor thought were responsible for her hallucinations, she still saw strange things and would peer around her room, complaining to Elsie that the room was full of people, insects, and mice.

Elsie, staying at night with her progressively more helpless mother, began to feel uneasy and had trouble sleeping in her mother's house.

When I'd get up to help her in the night I'd feel afraid to open the door to the upstairs, into the dark. Much less did I want to go up there. Like a little kid, I dreaded what might be behind closet doors, even though I scolded myself for letting what Mom was going through get to me. That is—until I had this terrible dream. . . .

Those nights I stayed with Mom I was sleeping on the sunporch, a long, narrow room with my bed at one end. One night, I thought I'd just waked up, and looking into the dark I saw this thing—something like a tiger with great talons—glaring at me. Leaping clear from the far end of the porch, it hit my bed so hard the bed rocked and shook. I screamed as loudly as I could and then, of course, I was instantly, really awake and the bed wasn't shaking at all.

I've read about a house where ghastly things happened to anyone living there, so some Christians went and prayed, to bind the evil spirits. I was sure something sinister was happening in my mother's house—I could feel an oppressive presence.

My folks' life without Christ, my daddy's interest in astrology, the pendulum, astral travel, and all his other occult dabbling—well, they opened a door for the demonic.

Daddy died a Christian, but at this point Mom had not become one. And I? I was so tense my own willpower couldn't get me to sleep. Even taking my problem to my prayer partners didn't get rid of my fear of Mom's house at night, but having prayer with someone who had been released from bondage to demonic forces by the Lord's intervention freed me from that paralyzing fear, although I still felt jittery, having to exert much self-control not to imagine lions under the bed. Only at my mother's house would I feel this fear; I'd get little jabs of "What if there *is* something up there?" Just enough to disturb the sleep I so badly needed.

One thing that helped was stumbling across Agnes Sanford's book, *The Healing Gifts of the Holy Spirit*, providentially tucked in among books on the occult at the library. The book helped me to formally renounce the devil and all his works, and to pray, "Lord, I don't want any other spirit besides Your Holy Spirit."

One night, as I struggled to overcome my fear, I thought—*I could pretend I'm sitting on God's lap the way I used to sit on Daddy's lap in the rocking chair when he'd read to me.* Just to get that feeling of support and protection I mentally pictured God as being a great big Father, and me as sitting on His lap. The bed under me, as I concentrated, became God's lap. The image, this healing thing, worked so well I went right to sleep.

Many times since, when I feel the least bit uneasy, I just ask God for comfort this way. It's good to have an imagination, especially a sanctified one. And it's not "just my imagination" because God really cares for us in this Fatherly way.

When I thought of letting God hold me on His lap, and put all my attention on the feeling of being supported, pretending it was not my bed but Him, I had no difficulty picturing Him and sensing His love surrounding me. I think we haven't begun to map what the brain can do—the brain He gave us.

David's Story

If King David could read Elsie's story he would probably say, "Yes, that is exactly the way it is."

When you read certain psalms along with his history as recorded in 1 and 2 Samuel, 1 Kings, and 1 Chronicles, you know that he, too, was often shaken by storms of doubt and fear before he finally made the safe harbor of total reliance on God. His cries for help in Psalms 57, 63, and 142 set a standard for candor every Christian would do well to follow.

When David hid in a cave, a fugitive from King Saul and his murdermania, he desperately summed up his plight, demanding that God *do* something. Later, his tone changed to quiet trust, as though his Lord had laid a calming hand on his shoulder. In Psalm 63, composed when David was hiding in the wilderness of Judah, "in a dry and weary land, where no water is," where asking for water or relief from fear would have seemed a reasonable request, David declared, instead:

*I will bless You while I live; I will lift up my hands in Your name
. . . my mouth shall praise You with joyful lips, When I remember
You upon my bed, and meditate on You in the night watches. For
You have been my help, and in the shadow of Your wings will I
rejoice.*

verses 4–7 AMP

At this crisis point David expresses no apprehension of what his
enemies might do to him. Instead, he focuses his attention on
God. Can't you imagine David on his bed after he has "meditated
on God in the night watches," finally turning on his side, closing
his eyes, and figuratively pulling God's "wings" up around
himself as he would a cloak, trustingly drifting off to sleep?

Whenever calamity struck, David followed the same pattern:
first, he turned to God for help (you get the feeling, reading the
Psalms, that it was a continuing, candid conversation), then he
did whatever he could to affect the circumstances, confident that
the God upon whom he called would listen and act.

A poignant example is seen in the tragic life of David's beloved
son, Absalom.

This young man, endowed with good looks, charm, wealth,
and prestige, caused his indulgent father intense sorrow by
plotting to wrest away the kingdom. Despite his grief at such
treachery, David did not rail at Absalom or at God. Instead, in
Psalms 4:8 (AMP), David, with great dignity, sets aside the hurt of
his heart, saying, "In peace I will both lie down and sleep, for
You, Lord, alone make me dwell in safety and confident trust."

Reading this psalm in conjunction with the tragedy of Absalom in 2 Samuel 15, you realize that David had every reason not
to be able to sleep. His burden of grief over his son's reckless

hatred that generated savage efforts to kill his father resounds painfully in the heart of every parent who has lain awake burning-eyed all night, asking, "Where did I fail?" and "Why does my child hate me, God?"

Not many parents are physically threatened by their children, but ingratitude or contempt or indifference or impatience wound the loving spirit as deeply as a dagger thrust. If you are a parent who knows this heart anguish, take comfort from David's example. During your ordeal, when living seems worse than dying could be, pour out all your pain and bewilderment to God, as honestly and bluntly, even crudely, as David did. Relief may not be instant, but when it comes it will last.

No chapter on fear of sleeping would be complete without a final thought about what sleep is—and isn't.

No one knows which ancient poet to blame for having first labeled sleep "a little death." From then on, writers and poets, in the manner of their kind, picked up that flawed thread and wove it inextricably into our literature. Today, many people believe unquestioningly that when we go to sleep we die a little. Some claim the Bible proves it, quoting Paul. True, he talked about death as being sleep, but he did *not* say sleep is a little death—a powerful difference.

How many anxious nonsleepers, enslaved by that implication, resist sleep unconsciously because they fear they may never wake up again, afraid this "little death" might slip over into the "big death"?

Under the burden of this fear, even the classic childhood prayer turns on us, like an affectionate cat, purring one moment and digging in very sharp claws and teeth the next:

Now I lay me down to sleep (Or is it to die?),
I pray the Lord my soul to keep (What if He doesn't exist after all?).
And if I die before I wake (What nothingness awaits?),
I pray the Lord my soul to take (Can I trust Him—if He is real?).

Far from being death, sleep merely resembles it. In a book titled *Somniquest*, evidence gathered in several sleep laboratories shows that as soon as your body settles in sleep, a great unseen activity begins.[13]

Your body is like an office building at night, after the workers have all gone home. Floor by floor the lights go off, various machines shut down, corridors echo emptily, elevators slumber in suspended animation. Then, gradually, a different kind of activity commences. Maintenance crews swarm over the building, repairing, cleaning, straightening, taking out the rubbish. Lights blaze and then click off as this army advances, room by room, to conquer daily clutter. The random workaholic who lingers late or comes in at odd hours finds himself unwelcome at the desk which during the day is his accredited station.

So with the person in sleep. Behind those closed eyes and supine body, mysterious activities begin. And in the mind?

Some students of sleep speculate that the weird and wonderful events we call dreams serve as safety valves deflating the pressures of life, cleaning out the mind in some way. Thus, after a restful night the body and mind, far from skirting "a little death," are rejuvenated, eager for another day.

If sleep is renewal time for body and mind, what about spiritual refreshment? In books about insomnia, this aspect of sleep is conspicuous by its absence. But doesn't it seem reasonable that the spirit, that indefinable essence of humanness, should also be renewed by sleep? And mightn't your attitude toward sleep influence your emotional/spiritual health as well?

In the holistic concept, the human being is not compartmentalized but is regarded as intricately interwoven, all parts fitting together. Present-day doctors, psychologists, and theologians are only now beginning to see how the body affects the mind-affects the spirit-affects the body in a Möbius Strip[14] only God could have created. Among the questions they must ask themselves is, "What does this mean for the insomniac?"

Scriptural evidence stipulates that God both gives and withholds sleep for His purposes. As over all else, He is the Ruler over sleep. In Job 33:15, Elihu tells Job: "In dreams, in visions of the night, when deepest sleep falls upon men . . . God makes them listen . . . " (NEB).

Also, we learn that sleep naturally follows obedience, as little as we like that word. The fatherly advice of Proverbs 3 is this: "My son, keep watch over your ability and prudence, do not let them slip from sight . . . when you lie down, your sleep will be pleasant" (verses 21–24 NEB).

If God were merely the Giver/Withholder of sleep, however, He would be a capricious master no better than the cruel pagan gods, but He is also our Protector and Guard. He has provided sleep as "a restorer of the soul"; He gives us the grace to trust Him for safety during sleep.

To help you accept the grace of a relaxed, trusting attitude toward God and His intentions for you, the next chapter invites you to think of God in another way—as your prescribing Physician.

If God were writing you a prescription for your sleepless nights, what do you suppose He would give you? Be assured, He offers a remedy far better than any sleeping pill. Let's see what happens when we transfer the trust we so freely bestow upon a fallible human physician to the Great Physician.

References and Suggested Midnight Reading

1. Alice K. Schwartz and Norma S. Aaron, "Anxiety Antidotes," *Somniquest: The Five Types of Sleeplessness and How to Overcome Them* (New York: Harmony Books, 1979).

2. Lester L. Coleman, M.D., column in the *Oregon Journal*, March 17, 1980.

3. Dietrich Langen, M.D., *Speaking of Sleeping Problems*, Medical Advisor Series (New York: Consolidated Book Publishers, 1978), p. 68.

4. Gay Gaer Luce and Dr. Julius Segal, *Insomnia* (New York: Doubleday & Co., Inc., 1969), p. 32.

5. See chapter 2, "Getting Your Mind Off Self and On God," section on brainstorming.

6. *Modern Maturity*, June/July 1981.

7. Norman Cousins, *Anatomy of an Illness* (New York: W.W. Norton & Co., Inc., 1979).

8. Ibid.

9. Ibid.

10. Luce and Segal, *Insomnia*, pp. 52 and following.

11. Phillip Goldberg and Daniel Kaufman, *Natural Sleep: How to Get Your Share* (Emmaus, Pennsylvania: Rodale Printing, Inc., 1978), p. 34.

12. See explanation of the RAS (Reticular Activating System) in chapter 8, "When God Writes the Prescription."

13. Schwartz and Aaron, *Somniquest*.

14. *The Random House Dictionary of the English Language*, unabridged edition (New York: Random House, 1973).

The Möbius Strip is a continuous, one-sided surface formed by twisting one end of a rectangular strip through 180 degrees about the longitudinal axis of the strip and attaching this end to the other.

Eight ★

When God Writes the Prescription

"Doctor, I'm having trouble sleeping—can you give me something?"

The doctor scribbles a prescription and we hurry to the pharmacy, expecting to feel better (to sleep again) as soon as that magic slip of paper is translated into equally magic pills.

We trust the pharmacist to decipher the doctor's hieroglyphics accurately. Such trust, based on need as much as on experience, depends on several intangibles: that both the physician and the pharmacist are sufficiently schooled and knowledgeable, that they possess goodwill and concern for us as individuals, and that they are zealous to heal. As patients, we display a touching trust—almost a religious belief. If we are insomniacs, our plea for "something—anything—to help me sleep" lacks only the bended knee and the folded hands to make it prayer.

The trouble is, most doctors will obligingly write a prescription for sleeping pills, even though authorities on sleeping problems now agree they are a nostrum to be avoided.

Doctor Dietrich Langen states unequivocally, "There is no such thing as a medicinal therapy against sleep disturbance."[1] Later, he asks rhetorically, "Is it wise permanently to suppress affective disturbances?"[2]

Translated from doctorese, this means, "What might be the consequences of always avoiding wakefulness, whatever the reasons?"

Doctor Langen then answers his own question: "The continued use of soporifics lames the switching function in the sleep-wakefulness mechanism." He continues, "Sleep so induced . . . is slight death . . . which is how sleep [itself] was formerly regarded."

His conclusion: "By hurling the body into sleep" these drugs can "make the organism [you or me] forget how to bring about sleep without the aid of sleeping pills."[3]

In *Natural Sleep*, Phillip Goldberg and Daniel Kaufman agree, describing the classic condition of sleeping pill habituation and including a list of the known side effects of their use. They warn, "These drugs do not induce natural sleep, they simply knock you out. . . ."[4]

Ironically, sleeping pills have one alarming side effect: for about two weeks they seem to be doing the job, then they *cause* insomnia.

And even if you sleep by taking pills, you can't win. Gay Gaer Luce and Dr. Julius Segal point to the "psychological effects of drug-taking—plus the emotional destruction from suppressing REM-delta sleep and the resultant nightmares."[5]

Isn't it time to recant our faith in a substance so perfidious?

In this decade, another reason for concern surfaced. One acclaimed sleeping pill, Dalmane, was found to be life-threatening to some elderly persons who may not know they have sleep apnea, that strange condition mentioned earlier, in which the sufferers literally cannot sleep and breathe at the same time. They may attribute their sleep difficulties to advancing age—which can be a fatal error.

Pharmacist/writer Joe Graedon warns, "Dalmane (flurazepam) lingers in the body and actually accumulates over time . . . a Stanford researcher reported that elderly patients suffered a dramatic increase in respiratory problems during sleep."[6]

Douglas Colligan's voice chimes in to call sleeping pills the "fast-food approach to insomnia" and mention that one-fifth of all doctor's office visits are made by people seeking sleeping pills. He, too, declares, "No pill gives you a completely normal night's sleep. . . ."[7]

Beyond that, Colligan adds an even more unsettling bit of information called "the one plus one equals three effect." He says:

> . . . prescription pills are too potent to mix with other similar drugs—sleeping pills, sedatives, tranquilizers or alcohol. The reason is something called . . . synergistics . . . in which the total effect of two or more drugs is greater than the sum of the combination's parts . . . that's one reason why using a little alcohol to wash down a sleeping pill can be a dangerous, almost suicidal habit.[8]

121

Disconcerting as it is to learn that the promised panacea is a menace, at least scientists have gleaned one valuable fact from all the sleep disorder detective work conducted during the past four decades. Informing us that sleeping pills and other such drugs, prescribed or plucked from self-service shelves in the drugstore, are counterproductive makes worthwhile every year and every dollar they spent in research.

First to go, then, must be "polypharmacy," that illogical American ritual of pill-popping. Luce and Segal agree that this presents a peculiar problem, however, for the doctor who knows most patients think he hasn't earned his fee unless he sends them out of his office clutching a prescription.[9]

Fortunately, more and more research expertise is focusing on sleep disorders; the number of institutions, clinics, and organizations studying it is increasing. In *Somniquest*, Alice Schwartz and Norma Aaron listed twenty-eight such institutions (pp. 211–213). In 1980, Quentin R. Regenstein, in *Sound Sleep*, revised that number to forty-nine, adding four from Canada and one in Belgium for good measure (pp. 185–194).

In 1988, Bruce Jordan, accreditation coordinator for the American Sleep Disorder Association* in Rochester, Minnesota, reported that in the United States alone the number has more than doubled to 110 accredited sleep disorder centers and 20 labs, the latter dealing only with sleep-related breathing problems such as sleep apnea.

But even after all the research is collated, synthesized, and run through the computer, something vital will still be missing. Unless the medical world listens to the religious world, they will

---

* American Sleep Disorder Association, 604 2nd Street SW, Rochester, MN 55902. Phone 1–507–287–6006.

not yet have put their hand on the essential lever. Most people in the medical community devoutly believe that medical/psychiatric remedies, which depend on analysis, logic, and the pragmatics of research, will eventually solve any dilemma, not excluding insomnia. You could say this is the "apostle's creed" of medicine. Along with Dr. Langen, most medical people are satisfied that sleep is "an instinct-related event that can be learned" (a contradiction in itself), and that we can "learn to live with functional hypnosomnia."[10]

So if the proper question is, "How can the doctor help the patient get back to sleep safely?" then reasonably speaking, answering that question *should* be medicine's goal. But what if scientists, not to mention most insomniacs, are asking the wrong question? What if doctors are treating the symptom, not the cause? What if the question they *should* be asking is, "How can the doctor help the patient use his wakefulness constructively?"

What if, without meaning to, doctors are thwarting God's purpose when He withholds sleep or wakes us up?

Without the balance spiritual insight brings to this dilemma, one day the drive to "get back to sleep" could lead down a very bizarre road. Scientists might one day condone the fantastic kind of sleep clinic described by Luce and Segal, where "people who are distraught will go to escape—for short vacations from life by prolonged sleep."[11]

Humanitarian as this may seem at first glance, the authors neglect to examine the possibility of such "vacations" becoming longer and longer until they deteriorate into an emotional creep back into the womb, or worse yet, into suicide without actual cessation of physical life. For the person whose stresses have grown into distresses so heavy to endure he/she craves sleep as escape, how easy it would be to succumb to such an enticement.

To be fair, the authors do not recommend establishing such a clinic. Furthermore, they say that no gadget for inducing sleep, like the "white noise machine," can equal "methods that can teach a person to become his/her own master . . . through modification of attitudes and habits."[12]

Applying our spiritual yardstick to their statement, we see that the Cross, to pun theologically, is still the crux of the matter. Without a new or renewed relationship with God through His Son, no amount of studying the biochemistry of sleep, or of devising bedtime rituals, or of practicing psychotherapeutic exercises for relaxation, will dig deep enough to uncover the root of the problem—despite the merits of each. No, the shiny new protégé of science, sleep disorder research, cannot of itself bring home the answer. Being your own master begins only when you yield your autonomy to the one Master, God, and obey His instructions for "modification of attitudes and habits."

Luce and Segal moved closer to the answer when they said, "No chemical can compete with what the mind can accomplish . . ." because in the mind/emotions (or call it "spirit") is precisely where God accomplishes some of His best work. Cooperating with Him, you can master your insomnia in a way not yet within the purview of physicians who treat their patients strictly according to the medical/chemical dialectic.

Regarding the successful treatment of insomnia, Luce and Segal insist, "No simple and universally applicable rules have yet been discovered by scientists." They are not aware that taming and harnessing that tiger of the night, insomnia, is not merely possible but guaranteed for those who realize God not only gives peace, He is Peace.

When Jesus said, "Come to Me . . . and I will give you rest . . ." He spoke words so rich with help for our human condition we could study that passage for a lifetime and never reach the end of its treasures. As we rest-hungry insomniacs look at His invitation, we know He has already proven Himself trustworthy, so we risk nothing if we take Him at His word. We don't go too far afield interpreting those words in Matthew, and others in John 15, as a prescription. Unlike the doctor's scribble, the Lord's message is perfectly legible; His divine pharmacopeia lies open before us.

By creatively grouping thoughts from Jesus' promises in John 15, we are able to receive His prescription for healing:

> *I am the Vine, you are the branches . . . cut off from vital union with Me—you can do nothing . . . [but] if you continue to obey My instructions [My prescription]—you will abide in My love. . . .*

John 15:5, 10 AMPLIFIED

How different from the usual instruction to "take two pills before bedtime."

Obeying this prescription from the Lord will produce infinitely better results than the sleeping pill unconsciousness that is like being hit on the head. Our whole spectrum of life will yield a rainbow of Love, Joy, Forbearance, Kindness, Goodness, Faithfulness, Humility, Self-control, and the special quality insomniacs so crave: Peace. In Paul's Letter to the Galatians (5:22), these side effects are called the "fruit of the Spirit," produced in us to nourish others as well as ourselves. As long as we obey His prescription to remain linked to Him, we will see these results in our lives. Jesus' promise is not a matter of "maybe this will help" but is powerful medicine capable of healing any hurt, including the restless spirit that won't let us find repose.

Challenge the idea of applying these passages to the insomnia problem if you wish; nevertheless, we want a marriage of medical terms and spiritual language that will transcend the usual. Bold thinking coupled with creative feelings opens new vistas of the mind and the spirit even as it upsets those who cling blindly to old meanings. Doesn't it seem worth a try to apply spiritual approaches to physical/medical problems?

A pioneering example of this was suggested by Marcine Vaswig, who works with her husband/pastor, Bill, in Preaching and Prayer Ministries/Life Institute.[13] She says that when you pray for someone's physical healing you should find out the specific condition being prayed for, from the person, a family member, or the attending physician. Thus, if an infection were the trouble, you would image the body area where war is being waged. Thinking of the white corpuscles as God's soldiers, you would picture them flooding the affected areas as the massed elements of His pure, white Light of Healing, asking Him to move into the battle zone with His power. It is of utmost importance, she emphasized, to know how the healing should be implemented, and how to image correctly. (Specifics for this approach have also been researched and practiced successfully from the medical standpoint by another husband/wife team, Carl and Stephanie Simonton.[14])

Use these basic principles: (1) know what is happening and how it must be approached in prayer, using the best medical/ diagnostic understanding; (2) translate the information into spiritual terms; (3) specify in your prayer your desire to commit the problem into God's hands. You can bring your sleepless condition under control.

But first learn how the brain works regarding sleep.

In "The Brain and the Phenomenon of Consciousness," psychologist/therapist D. Robert Lindberg, Ph.D., describes the RAS—the Reticular Activating System. Of this awake-not awake system in our midbrain, he says, "When this system is 'on' we are awake; when 'off' we no longer have waking consciousness."

He adds, "It is a vast network (reticulum) of cells in our midbrain which has the capacity to determine which messages should get through to our cortex at any given moment, and which ones should wait."[15]

At one point Dr. Lindberg startled me considerably when he opened up a new perception of will and obedience. He posed the question, "Who controls the RAS?"

I had assumed that anything to do with the brain was not within my power to control because thought happens so quickly. Like a computer, I reasoned, once on—it just goes.

He explains:

Most human beings discover . . . that they *choose* what they want to be conscious of and reject all else at a given moment . . . thousands of things in life "demand" our attention . . . our own inner "voices" of memory, emotions, and desires.

How liberating to learn we control our own RAS, but beyond that, to realize an even greater freedom awaits. As soon as we yield our own will to God's will and rely on His direction, our will melded with His, the moment-by-moment decision to stay awake or go to sleep becomes easier. Confronted by a problem that is keeping us awake, we can say to God, "Shall I stay awake and work this out, or is it something You will take care of, so I might as well go to sleep?"

Giving up what we regard as ours seems difficult, but the resulting peace far outstrips whatever transient satisfaction being in total charge of ourselves can bring. In submission to Him, we receive from Him an undreamed-of ability to control our own RAS. We break through into a new dimension contained in the familiar words, ". . . whoever loses his life . . . for My sake, shall find [life everlasting]" (Matthew 16:25 AMPLIFIED). The more we submit to God, the more we are *able* to submit to Him.

Translating physiological information into spiritual terms subjects our RAS to the same practice we, as Christians, follow in other areas of our lives whenever we say, "According to Your will, Lord, let it be for me."

Serenely, we can wait on God's purpose for our sleeping problems, and if we fall again into the old rut of worrying about not sleeping—and this can happen even though we have given it to the Lord—we can then pray without any false guilt:

Thank You, Lord, for taking over my problem. What a relief to know You will handle it in the way best for me. Thank You for reminding me I don't struggle alone whenever I tangle myself in worry.

If you desire to be like the One who said, ". . . yet not My will, but . . . Yours, be done" (Luke 22:42 AMPLIFIED), you are learning, not to instruct God in how to answer your requests, but to want whatever He wants for you. Go or stay, live or die, sleep or stay awake—ideally your most earnest prayer is for strength to want to be found within His will. Thus the student in God's night school prays:

> Lord, if You want me to, I'll stay awake all night, trusting You to give me the strength to work tomorrow without having slept. If You give me sleep, I will accept it with thanks. If You do not give me sleep, I will simply wait, resting, on You. Thank You for giving me the faith to pray this way. Let all be according to Your will.

This prepares you for the next step. Picture your midbrain, imagining its third relay switch, the RAS. Although no one understands exactly how this complicated system works, for the sake of having some sort of picture, use the analog of an instrument panel with many delicately balanced switches. On the TV screen of your mind image the words *choose, reject, store,* and *"override"* on these switches. They represent choices you make every moment, exercising control over the system. If, as Dr. Lindberg maintains, you can "take over control . . . at any time and in any degree [you] wish . . . a capacity of voluntary control . . . subject to our continued effort [which] improves with practice," you are now ready for the next step, which is to pray the following:

> Master, I give control of my RAS over to You. I relinquish control of those relay switches in my midbrain because I want to be totally obedient—mind/body/spirit. Please instruct my RAS to work according to Your commands. In particular, direct my choices about sleep. Help me know how to act in obedience to Your will.

As you think about those instructions, listen to another of Dr. Lindberg's apperceptive conclusions: "Whenever we press ourselves to our supposed limits, those limits themselves are extended."[16]

Might this imply that God waits for us to press against the limits of our supposed capabilities so He can extend them? Is it possible that by using commonplace denial or rejection mechanisms we can frustrate—or aid—God's intent to help us grow?

Who hasn't called a meeting of the original committee mentioned earlier—the Me, Myself, and I committee—to argue out an issue.

Me: I've got to get some sleep . . . well, I'll just use some of these sleeping pills the doctor gave me.

Myself: Don't you remember—that might be dangerous.

I: I agree with Me; I *must* sleep.

Me: Well—maybe if I work until I'm exhausted, I'll fall asleep as soon as my head hits the pillow.

Myself: Huh. Who are you trying to fool? It didn't work the last six times you tried it.

I: It's not fair—everybody else can sleep. . . .

Me: Okay, how about this—I could read or watch TV until I get sleepy.

Myself: Hmmm—that might do it, but it probably won't work either.

I: Yeah, but it's a good excuse to watch Johnny and then tomorrow when I go to work with big black circles under my eyes I'll have an excuse to goof off.

Me: I can't understand it—why is God doing this to me?

Myself: Why don't you ask Him?

I: No—don't! I—I'm not sure I want to hear His answer.

Me: Well, somebody must know why I can't sleep.

Myself: Let's face it—I have a lot on my mind—you know, that sticky situation with—

I: Maybe I'll just have to face up to my mistakes—quit blaming others—stop pretending they aren't my own fault and figure out how to turn my life around. . . .

Now contrast this confusion of interior counselors with acceptance of wakefulness, having turned the whole thing over to God. Alert, yet relaxed and ready to hear whatever the Lord prescribes, our anxiety about getting to sleep diminishes in direct ratio to our realization that sleep is not the most important event in life.

Rest, revealed in all its deeper meanings as being of supreme importance, comes as a result of following the prescription God offers. And if we still shrink from pressing ourselves beyond self-perceived limits, He will lovingly do it for us. When we finally reconcile to involuntary wakefulness as within His perfect rationale for us, we are given the grace to regard ourselves as wake*full* rather than as sleep*less*, with all that implies. When that happens, we will have broken through the barrier between ourselves and the spiritual growth our Father wants for us.

In His wisdom, God knows that we must grow spiritually in order to achieve mental and emotional maturity. When those standards are met, total health results. God sees the person as well as the patient. Isn't it high time doctors, instead of reflexively writing a prescription, did the same? If this happens, we will begin to see prognoses being made on the basis of the needs of "human beings in whom disease exists" or in whom trauma has taken over the life.

A broken leg, for instance, can efficiently be set and put on the way to mending, but if mental/emotional distress is ignored, even the knitting together of the bone can be delayed. Those who have dragged around a walking cast know all too well the accompanying stress. They want and need spiritual/philosophical help as much as they need relief from the initial physical pain.

Of course, the person/patient must cooperate with the doctor. Whether a broken leg or sleepless nights are complicating life, some radical changes must be made. The insomniac who never before regarded wakefulness as a good thing will have to discard old thought patterns.

It's a matter of trust, whether you are trusting your doctor—or God. When you get a prescription from your family physician, you read the directions and scrupulously follow them. It would be foolish to do otherwise because not only would you waste your money but you also might not get the good from the medication. To "take according to directions" is vital.

God, too, writes prescriptions. In chapter 9, some interpretations of His prescriptions are offered to help you. Given in the form of spiritual exercises—Bible study, self-examination, writing in a journal, and meditation—they can equip you for facing wakeful nights with anticipation and aplomb.

Because meditation is a controversial exercise by some standards and an unknown quantity by others, before you begin the chapter ask yourself what meditation is. If your answer reveals that you are wary and curious, or draw a blank but are not unwilling to learn, read on.

References and Suggested Midnight Reading

1. Dietrich Langen, M.D., *Speaking of Sleeping Problems*, Medical Advisor Series (New York: Consolidated Book Publishers, 1978), p. 102.

2. Ibid., p. 107.

3. Ibid., p. 109.

4. Phillip Goldberg and Daniel Kaufman, *Natural Sleep: How to Get Your Share* (Emmaus, Pennsylvania: Rodale Printing, Inc., 1978) pp. 47, 50, 56.

5. Gay Gaer Luce and Dr. Julius Segal, *Insomnia* (New York: Doubleday & Co., Inc., 1969).

6. Joe Graedon, "People's Pharmacy" column in the *Oregon Journal*, August 19, 1982.

7. Douglas Colligan, *Creative Insomnia* (New York: McGraw-Hill Book Company, 1978), pp. 78, 79.

8. Ibid., p. 84.

9. Luce and Segal, *Insomnia*, pp. 224 and following.

10. Langen, *Sleeping Problems*, p. 66.

11. Luce and Segal, *Insomnia*, pp. 224 and following.

12. Ibid.

13. William (Pastor Bill) Vaswig and Marcine Vaswig
Preaching and Prayer Ministries/Life Institute
1406 140th Place Northeast, #107
Bellevue, WA 98007

14. O. Carl Simonton, M.D., Stephanie Matthews-Simonton, and James L. Creighton, *Getting Well Again* (Los Angeles: Jeremy P. Tarcher, Inc., 1978).

15. D. Robert Lindberg, Ph.D., "The Brain and the Phenomenon of Consciousness." Unpublished article.

16. Ibid.

Nine ★

Seven Spiritual Exercises for Wide-Awake Nights*

NOTE: Meditation is like a waking dream, a valid substitute for the REM-state dreams you cannot achieve, being sleepless.

However, meditation in the Christian sense is far different from the practices Eastern religions promulgate. For your spiritual safety, a comparison of transcendental meditation (TM) and Christian meditation (CM) follows.

POINT ONE: *Transcendental meditation* scorns the mind, relying on the *mantra*, which is the mental use of spoken sounds without meaning for the user, an elimination of all consciously directed thoughts. The Guru Maharaj Ji, of the Divine Light

* These exercises need not be limited to sleepless nights. Anyone can benefit from using them as part of devotional life—day or night.

Mission, teaches, "In order to obtain 'True Knowledge,' one must bypass the mind."[1] The guru also maintains that the human mind is little more than garbage.

In regard to this, David Haddon warns:

The first hazard of the mystical experience via mantramic technique is that it blinds the mind to the truth of the gospel by displacing reason . . . opens the mind to false ideas about God and reality. [It] is the doorway to the mystical enlightenment on which the false doctrines of Hindu monism, the Buddhist concept of the primacy of the Void, have been built.[2]

He adds that the passive mental state ". . . opens the way for unrecognized demonic influence [that] may make rejection of false spiritual practices difficult, even for [Christian] believers."[3]

Christian meditation, on the other hand, puts the human "logos" or reason in touch with Divine Logos, Christ the Rational Principle Incarnate. Through reading the Bible and seeking God's presence during meditation, the whole being is flooded with His Light and with the healing and redirecting power of His Holy Spirit.

As Haddon says, "An obedient sensitivity to the Spirit when He shows the believer how God's Word applies to life is the basis of the discipline."[4]

POINT TWO: TM, according to the movement's own litera-ture as reported in *Natural Sleep*, is ". . . easy . . . requires no particular level of commitment or understanding," but neverthe-less, ". . . must be learned through private instruction by a qualified teacher."[5]

Both the TM people and the *Natural Sleep* authors, Phillip Goldberg and Daniel Kaufman, issue strong warnings against independent use of the mantra. Oddly enough, it soon appears that only those who are the disciples of the Hindu monk Maharishi Mahesh Yogi are qualified to teach.

Goldberg and Kaufman advise readers to "invest the time and money in the TM standard course. . . ." (In 1978, the cost of a TM course was $165, with "extensive follow-up as needed.")[6] Ten years later a more sophisticated tier of charges for their seven-step process includes $600 per family, including children; $400 for regularly employed persons; $75 for students. * All this for a technique the teachers promise is "automatic, natural, effortless."

Think of the *biblical contrast* in Isaiah 55:1 (AMP): "Wait and listen, every one who is thirsty! . . . he who has no money, come, buy and eat! Yes, come, buy priceless [spiritual] wine and milk without money. . . ." And think of Jesus' promise in John 7:37, 38: "If any man is thirsty, let him come to Me and drink! He who believes in Me. . . . Out from his innermost being springs and rivers of living water shall flow."

When you open your mind in Christian meditation (CM), you do not expose yourself to "whatever"; you put your whole self into the safekeeping of God. At this most vulnerable time, you are like a fledgling bird fresh out of the egg; you need the covering wing of God to protect you from the Enemy.

POINT THREE: As important as the first two points are, the third must take precedence. Listen as the proponents of TM, Goldberg and Kaufman, continue:

> During private instruction, the TM teacher assigns a mantra individually, according to certain criteria which he will not

* Source: Portland Transcendental Meditation Program, 1822 SW Madison, Portland, OR 97205–1717.

divulge. The teacher then guides the student in proper use of the mantra . . . instructions for its use are matters of precision requiring training.[7]

These "meaningless words" given, on the student's pledge of secrecy, to be repeated until they become unrelated sounds seem harmless enough, but Spiritual Counterfeits Projects researchers disagree. They advise, ". . . each [mantra] is the name of a Hindu deity, a vehicle to the spirit world. . . ."[8]

Eventually, the person learning to be a TM meditator is asked to take part in a little ceremony. The initiate must bring a white handkerchief or a flower, assured that this is merely a token. Actually, he/she is laying an offering before Hindu gods and, repeating the personal mantra as required, thinks this is a nice little graduation exercise—but he/she is actually taking part in worship of those gods.

Any Christian immediately recognizes shocking implications. God's command is, "You shall have no other gods before or besides Me" (Exodus 20:3 AMP).

In CM, no such subterfuge is used. The meditator frankly seeks the presence of the God of Abraham, Isaac, and Jacob, the Father of our Lord Jesus, the Christ, whether by reading the Bible or by entering a prayerful state using his/her logos, that active application of the power of reason given to humankind by God.

David Haddon says:

The mantramic technique . . . suppresses not only the meaning inherent in the word[s] of the mantra, but also the generation of any thought in the mind by its user . . . word, thought and mind are all suppressed. . . .[9]

But when you use CM, instead of repeating a word until it is stripped of its meaning, you focus your attention on the goodness of God, on His love as shown in Christ's Passion, or on any other of His magnificent attributes. Applying mind as well as emotions, you "center down" on God. Keenly comprehending the meanings of the words you say or think, stimulated by the Holy Spirit, your logos thrives and the insights you receive nourish your whole being. Looking to God alone for help, you testify to His sovereignty in your life.

Rather than offering you an anodyne like the mantra, which disconnects you from reality by numbing your mind, the Lord invites you to know and vigorously comprehend the rich meanings of every word you speak, every thought you think about His wonderful Fatherhood. You are obeying Jesus' command: "You shall love the Lord your God with all your heart, and with all your soul, and *with all your mind*" (Matthew 22:37 AMPLIFIED, emphasis added).

Are you ready to try Christian meditation? Only one more point needs to be clarified.

In his book *At Your Word, Lord*, William Vaswig gives ideal prayer time advice.[10] Try this variation of Pastor Bill's Pattern of Protection and use it at the beginning of each exercise:

> *Father, as Your adopted son/daughter, I claim*
> *the privilege in Jesus' Name to say,*
> *I seal myself with the sign of the Cross.*
> *(Sign a cross in the air.)*
>
> *I cover myself with the Blood of Jesus Christ.*
> *(Make a sweeping motion from head to foot.)*

*I circle myself with the light of Your Presence
so nothing can come through to harm me.
(Draw a circle in the air all the way around yourself.)*

All this I claim in the power of Your Holy Spirit. Amen.

By thus making a straight path between yourself and the Lord, you invite Him to sweep it clean of dark and hostile forces. You are actively using your intellect with God's approval and opening yourself to an intimate time with Him during your bonus midnight hours.

Exercise #1 A Directed Meditation

Tonight, instead of lying there in bed staring sleeplessly into the dark, get up and go to a place where you can be alone, with the light on. If a disability keeps you in bed, alter the following directions in whatever way fits your situation.

Have ready a notebook in which you will start your Midnight Journal (if you haven't already done so), and a lighted candle. A votive candle in its glass cup is safest. Tonight will be a meditation exercise, so turn off the electric light for now. (You may wish to read through the exercises beforehand or put them on tape so you can concentrate on doing them while listening to your own voice.)

Following the Pattern of Protection, or your own version, sit quietly and think about the Cross, the covering Blood, the shimmering circle of God Light surrounding you, and thank the Heavenly Father that no evil can penetrate your refuge.

Next, use this Tense/Relax routine, closing your eyes for better concentration:

- Sit on a straight chair, feet flat on the floor, hands lying open in your lap.
- Beginning with your feet, tighten the muscles of your toes and the arches of your feet for five slow counts, then relax.
- Next, think about the muscles of your calves; do the same.
- In thought, move to your knees and thighs; tense for five slow counts, relax.
- Do the same for your hips, then the muscles of your abdomen, the small of your back, chest, rib cage, and shoulders.
- Think about your hands; clench your fists as hard as you can, then slowly let your hands fall open again.
- Tense your forearms and upper arms, working up toward your shoulders.
- Lay back your ears like an angry cat, count to five, relax. (This may surprise you. Most people don't know they tense their ears and scalp under stress.)
- When you relax, note the loosening of your neck and scalp as well as the muscles around your ears.
- Next, stick out your tongue as though trying to touch your chin, count to five, relax.
- Frown as hard as you can, pulling all the muscles of your face into a scowl, count five and relax. If this strikes you as funny so much the better.
- Sit a few moments longer, checking mentally for any other tense muscles, doing the same for each.

Open your eyes now and look at the candle flame. Appreciate its subtle colors; observe how this tiny light reveals the room. As you think about the power of this fragile thing, recall that Jesus says we are to be light. Even a little light like this candle, touched by His Light, cannot be blown out but brings hope into darkness.

Eyes closed again, "image" Jesus from your favorite mental concept or artist's depiction. To do this, see Him as being as real and solid as yourself. By the power of your imagination, bring Him into the room. Feel the air stir as He comes in and sits down beside you. Greet Him, see His answering smile, and feel the firm grip of His hand. Let the resonance of His deep voice vibrate all through your body. Lay your hand without fear on His sleeve, feel the rough texture of His robe and His strong arm beneath. . . .

In the same way you imaged Jesus, think of someone near to you with whom you are not in harmony. In detail, think of his/her unique qualities, distinctive tones of voice, little idiosyncrasies, habits of conversation, the ties that bind you together, the differences that separate you. . . .

Imagine the person now coming into the room and sitting down at the table with you and Jesus. Try for eye contact and look at the person as though you had just met. If you were not carrying a load of emotional baggage, how would you act? What impressions would you want to make? . . .

If this is a relationship of long standing, recall what drew you together in the first place. Ask yourself if the person still has those qualities. Ask yourself if you retain the qualities the other person found attractive. . . .

Turn to Jesus and ask Him to help you and the other person find those answers. As the three of you sit quietly together, let Jesus' goodness and peace flow freely. Let His Light trim the flickering wick of your little light. Look now at the other person, letting your fears and resentments drop away in the radiance of Jesus. . . .

Let the truth sink deep into your mind: Jesus understands every aspect of your relationship, so you needn't explain or defend or complain. Being here with Him, letting His love heal the wounds, is enough for now. . . .

Jesus stretches out His hands to you both; clasp His hand on one side, the hand of the person you need to be reconciled with on the other, to form a linked circle. As you feel the warm strength of Jesus' hand and the tentative touch of the other person's, let the Lord's life and love pulse through you freely, bringing forgiveness and new resolve to do whatever is needed to let the Christ Light dispel the shadows between you. . . .

Remain in your circle as long as you wish. When it is time for Jesus and the other person to leave, hug them both if you want to. (You always remain in control of whatever happens in an imaging meditation, but don't be surprised if something happens you had not planned. Let it happen or not, as you wish.)

Alone again, look at the candle and slowly return to your awareness of the night and your surroundings.

Take a few moments to record your impressions in your journal, dating the entry. Blow our your candle and—good night.

Exercise #2 Promises of Blessing (Bible Study and Meditation)

Are you alarmed because you are awake again tonight? You needn't be. Breaking the habit of considering yourself sleep*less* takes time. Soon you will see how these wake*ful* times can become full indeed—of blessings.

Go now to the place you've chosen for your rendezvous with God. You will need the light on but also light a candle if it is a comfort to you. If you prefer not to have a lighted candle nearby, simply thank Jesus for being your Light in the night.

Seek God's protection, using the Vaswig Pattern given in Exercise #1, or your own variation. . . .

Think now about the word *blessing*. In your journal write what it means to you, then look it up in the dictionary and add that definition to your own. Note also the definitions of *blessed* and *bless*.

Read the nine beatitudes of Jesus (Matthew 5:3–12), if possible in the Amplified Bible. Soak yourself in the promises of "blessedness" or "happiness."

Record any fresh insight or new perspective in your journal. Date all entries—day/month/year.

In a concordance, look up verses containing those three words and write them down. Notice how *blessed* and *happy* can often be used interchangeably.

Because there are a great many such verses, you may wish to make this a regular feature of your devotions, whether daily or nightly. Follow your own inner directive.

After you have written down several verses which use "bless," "blessed," or "blessing" and your responses, lay aside your pen and employ the Tense/Relax routine given in Exercise #1. When you are relaxed, turn your attention to the candle flame, letting your thoughts drift wherever they want to go. . . .

Before doing this, click off the light; quietly ask God to shine into your mind and heart the way the candle shines in the dark room. . . .

If you are watching a candle in your mind instead, thank Him for the imagination He has given you to do so. . . .

Think of the way the candle burns. It doesn't *try* to burn, it simply burns. Use that as a guide as you think about the verses you wrote down . . . think of the ways God's Light, Jesus, lights

144

our way through the darkness. . . . Let Him light your darkness. . . .

If stress-making thoughts creep back in, allow them to come, but don't welcome them by worrying. Calmly give each one to God, thanking Him because you know you needn't deal with them alone. . . .

Think of yourself as a rock in the middle of a mountain brook, sitting solid and serene. Regard those stressful thoughts as water rushing and foaming around and over you but having no effect on you. Twigs, leaves, and other litter of anxiety flow on past you down the stream of life. . . .

Ask God to show you how insomnia can be a blessing, remembering Jesus' words: "Keep on asking and it will be given you; keep on seeking and you will find; keep on knocking and the door will be opened to you" (Matthew 7:7; *see also* Luke 11:9 AMPLIFIED).

In this time of sitting quietly, you are making yourself available to God, perhaps as never before. . . .

Think about God's desire to bless you. Believe He wants only the best for you, that any task He gives you will glorify Him and give your life new purpose. . . .

When you are ready, slowly begin moving, first your hands and feet, then the rest of your body, returning to full awareness of your surroundings. Click your light on and sit a few moments thinking about your Father. . . .

You may wish to write a prayer of thanks for His care and love, and to commemorate this moment. If so, think along these lines:

Dear Lord, thank You for showing me how insomnia can be a blessing. The more I think of it this way the less threatening being awake at night seems.

-or-

Dear Father, I don't yet see how insomnia can be a blessing, but I'm willing to learn. At least I can now think about it without fear. Reading verses about being blessed or happy seems to help.

-or-

Father, thank You for being here now with me. As I seek to make sense of my insomnia by reading Your Book, I realize that You are the Word in Your Son. You bring truth and hope to me.

I am beginning to *feel* blessed by thinking it through with You and willing my belief. As an act of will, I claim Your promise of blessing.

As you snuff your candle and put away your writing things, be assured that God can give you a good night whether or not you sleep. He can give you all the energy you need to face the coming day. He can give you mastery of your insomnia.

Exercise #3 Peace and Safety (A Meditation)

By now, your former distress at being awake may be giving way to curiosity. You may even be looking forward to this late-night meeting with God. Perhaps you wonder, *What's God going to show me tonight?*

As you settle in your accustomed place, you should have your Bible and journal handy, but chances are you won't use them.

Light your candle as a reminder that Jesus is the Light and that this is a special time for seeing what His Light will reveal. Ask for God's protection, using the Vaswig Protection Pattern. Turn off the electric light; let your body relax and be still. As before, sit on a straight chair and employ the Tense/Relax routine. If you are in bed, rest back against your pillows in whatever way is most comfortable. If you are having pain, offer your need for healing—of body/mind/spirit—to God. Believe Him for the healing that even now is taking place. . . .

Center your eyes and thoughts on the candle flame. As you watch it burn, cherish its fragile beauty as you ponder its awesome power. A tiny spark of fire can destroy a mighty forest—or bring light into the darkness of despair.

Thinking of Jesus as that Light, believe that God has called you to this session. Offer thanks, calling on Him by whatever name seems most appropriate—however you perceive Him. Tell Him you know He is present. You may not "feel" His presence but you can believe He is here because He says:

> . . . *I will not in any way fail you nor give you up nor leave you without support. [I will] not, [I will] not, [I will] not in any degree leave you helpless, nor forsake nor let [you] down. . . . Assuredly not!*

> Hebrews 13:5 AMPLIFIED

As you draw near to God by this act of faith and will, He will reveal how near He is to you (James 4:8).

Still watching the candle flame, thank Him for His faithfulness and for other blessings you have received but perhaps hadn't noticed until now.

If worrisome thoughts intrude again, give yourself permission not to deal with them right now. Firmly, gently, center your attention always on that candle flame, as a reminder of Christ shining into the dark world and also into the dark corners of your mind, where shapes and shadows lurk. He will banish all the "what ifs" that frighten you.

Now notice your breathing and think about how breathing—in and out—in and out—is also a blessing from God. As you breathe, meditate this way, accenting the italicized words:

All will be well
    All *will* be well
        All will *be* well
            All will be *well*—for God is here.

Now say these phrases aloud (if only in a whisper), letting them enter your being with each indrawn breath. As you exhale, say the phrases again. . . .

With each indrawn breath, savor every word as the breath of life. Let the phrases, one after another, penetrate your being the way air penetrates your lungs. . . .

With each expelled breath, think of the worries and anxieties going out of your body like a mist. Watch that mist disappear into the candle flame. Quietly think of the flame as Jesus. . . .

Repeat these four lines for as long as you wish. . . .

Notice how your body relaxes, your mind tumult hushes, your breathing slows, and your heart responds with a more regular beat, as you give yourself completely to this healing. . . .

Sit as long as it takes for the sense of peace, the Presence of the Holy Spirit, to pervade your consciousness. . . .

Now, slowly begin to move and flex your hands and legs, then the rest of your body, and to come back to everyday (night) reality.

If you wish, record your impressions in your journal and thank God for this time with Him, knowing you can repeat it anytime you want to. As you snuff your candle and put your things away, know that you can rest well—you are safe.

Exercise #4 Release From Guilt (A Meditation)

If this is the fourth night you've been awake, you have probably realized that you are a student in God's night school. Tonight's is a very special session.

On previous nights, you established a place to be and learned to have certain things on hand for these sessions. Tonight, add a metal wastebasket or other metal container.

After you have lighted your candle, make yourself comfortable following the Tense/Relax method. Remembering that every muscle in your body needs a chance to relax, begin at your feet and work your way up. Don't forget the muscles of your face, your forehead, and around your ears. . . .

This relaxation technique works best if you sit on a straight chair with feet flat on the floor—no crossed legs or legs wound around the chair legs. Check over your entire body until you feel loose and easy.

Thinking of the candle flame as symbolic of God's Light in the world, and in your world particularly, let His Light flow into any relationships that have caused or are causing you distress. . . . Do not try to solve them at this time. Just mark them in your mind as pending and concentrate on letting the Christ Light shine into every nook and cranny of your life. Think of it as opening the door on the first warm day of spring, to let a flood of sunshine (Sonshine) into your winter/life. Be sure you don't block the Light with excuses or explanations. . . .

Take as long as you need. If one situation or relationship seems to monopolize your attention, let Christ's Light shine most steadily there. If your attention wavers, look again at the candle to help you "center down." . . .

When you feel that you have your list well in mind, move gradually out of the meditative state as you have learned to do, and prepare for the next stage of this exercise.

You've had the electric light out; now turn it back on. Put your list on paper. Opposite each item, list any way(s) you may have been responsible for the problem between you and another. Be as honest as you can; this is for your eyes only. Also be as kind to yourself as you would want someone else to be.

Allow yourself to feel whatever you feel. John Powell, author of *Why Am I Afraid to Tell You Who I Am?* says we should never deny our feelings but instead should center our energies on acting out those feelings in acceptable ways. Talk out loud (or stage whisper) about your feelings if it helps—but no primal screams, please.

Offer your feelings and emotions to God—good and bad—knowing He accepts you just as you are. . . .

Ask Him to forgive you for your part in causing the problem, freely admitting your failures and faults without excuse. . . .

Now ask Him to forgive others for their part in the problem. You needn't make accusations; God will dispense both justice and mercy. . . .

When you have given as much of your problem to the Lord as you are able, thank Him for taking your burden. If you realize later that you are still harboring resentment or guilt or hatred, again thank Him for taking your burden. This way you will remind yourself that He has lifted it from you, and you will also refresh your faith that this is so.

Thank God for His readiness to forgive and forget. Ask Him for the strength to do the same. If you feel it is impossible for you to forgive, ask Jesus to let His Calvary forgiveness flow through you. In this way you and the person you need to forgive, who also needs to forgive you, may both be forgiven by Him.

Taking your list of grievances and confessed sins, carefully touch it to the lighted candle, the symbol of God's purifying love, and drop the burning list into the metal container.

As you watch your list of miseries burn away to ashes, pray in this manner:

Dear Father, thank You for wiping out all my fears, guilt, anger, and resentment as totally as the fire is burning up this paper. The candle flame and the burning paper remind me of Your Son, who brought the radiance of Your love, the consuming heat of Your love, and the cleansing power of Your love that now restores me to my place as Your child. Show me, Father, what You want me to do next. So let it be, in Your Firstborn's Name.

If you should still feel not at rest, go back and follow the directions again, asking God to help you accept your real feelings. If you are angry, or fear something you can't identify, ask God the Holy Spirit to bring the reason up out of your unconscious without harm or pain, so that you and He can deal with it. . . .

Whether or not catharsis takes place, thank God; believe Him for continued healing and protection. As you snuff the candle, claim the Jesus Flame burning in your heart as your night-light, and go back to bed.

Exercise #5 Transposing (Bible Study in Your Own "Key")

In this exercise you will learn how to transpose. By taking a verse of the Bible and looking at it in a new way, you will change it into your own "key" much the way a singer transposes music into his/her own singing range. Your transpositions will be as different from anyone else's as you are from every other person in the world. Thus, there is no right or wrong way to do it.

Transposing lifts the words of Scripture out of the remote (events that may have happened long ago to unreal characters), making them intimate promises and immediate surprises planned as though exclusively for you.

Just waiting for you to find them are love songs from God which begin, "Dear [your name]." Transposing can be your nightsong offered back to Him.

By now you go straight to the part of the house where you can have a light on. You have your Bible and journal at hand. If you enjoy the cheerful glow of a candle, light it now.

Follow the familiar routines of Protection and Tense/Relax. Don't forget the muscles of your face and neck, and across the tops of your shoulders. Scrunching up your face as tight as you can and then relaxing all those tight muscles for five slow counts will smooth out frown marks and help unclench your teeth. . . .

Let your mind/spirit relax, too, by listening to the night. Revel in the freedom from interruptions and thank God for the muteness of the tyrant telephone. No one needs you at this moment, unless you have a baby in the house. If so, ask God to help the baby sleep peacefully for now. . . .

To make this interlude perfect, let go any anxiety you may have about the lateness of the hour. Remember that the purpose of this time with God is not so much to get back to sleep as to let Him show you how to use your wakefulness.

Try not to set a time limit on how long you will be involved with this exercise. God will let you know when class is dismissed.

As you look for His personal messages to you in His Book, ask Him to bring His Light into your mind and heart. Ask Him to teach you how to transpose those messages into your own key. Ask Him to help you recognize the verses containing His Word for you. . . .

Set aside, for now, previous understanding of familiar verses. Pretend you have never seen them before. If possible, use a translation new to you.

When you transpose, you are not composing a new translation—you are simply claiming the helps in terms you can understand. Expect to receive new insights. You won't be disappointed.

Some verses will transpose easily; some will speak to you or even sing, while others will remain silent. Those which move you deeply will bless your life in ways you cannot now imagine.

Before you look for these messages, pray:

Dear Jesus, thank You for being here now with me as I look for solutions for my insomnia by reading Your Word. I know You are the Living Word; I know I can trust every word You say or show me in Your Book.

Listen for a breath or two, because the Lord may want to reply. . . .

Think of a favorite verse; write it in your journal. One of my favorites, since I learned to transpose, is Psalms 34:8 (AMP):

> O taste and see that the Lord [our God] is good! Blessed . . . is the man [woman] who trusts and takes refuge in Him.

Beautiful? Yes, but impersonal. This declaration springs to life when you transpose it to this:

> Oh Lord, You taste so good! And I feel so much more relaxed since I began to trust You, to come to You first when I need a safe place.

Friends who have read this transposition did not agree with my interpretation (transposition), but that's all right. They are free to make their own, as long as it is true to the spirit of the text.

Transposing is merely taking personally the promises, rebukes, admonitions, commands, and comforts in the Bible. Do not hesitate to believe that just as He spoke to ordinary people when He walked the hills of Galilee, He is speaking to you, now.

Another portion—John 3:16—brings a powerful message of hope to me when it is transposed. Try this: Every place the verse says "world" put your own name, i.e., "For God so greatly loved and dearly prized [your name] that He [even] gave up His only-begotten Son, so that if [your name] believes in . . . Him [he/she] shall not perish—come to destruction, be lost—but have eternal . . . life" (AMPLIFIED).

Verse 17: "For God did not send the Son to [your name] in order to judge—to reject, to condemn, to pass sentence on—[your name]; but that [your name] might find salvation and be made safe and sound through Him" (AMPLIFIED).

Write out those two verses with your own name in place and see what a strengthening it can be for you.

A longer passage might help you as it has helped me— Matthew 5:6 in the Amplified Bible:

> *Blessed and fortunate and happy and spiritually prosperous [that is, in that state in which the born-again child of God enjoys His favor and salvation] are those who hunger and thirst for righteousness (uprightness and right standing with God), for they shall be completely satisfied!*

It is a challenge to transpose, but what about this:

> Lord, I came to You hungry and thirsty for righteousness, yearning above all to be in right standing with You as Your child. At once, You showered extravagant blessings on me in a never-ending stream. Even when I feel bankrupt spiritually, You remind me that I am Your child. Then I am content.

Let your own transposition speak your response to this marvelous promise and then claim it the way you would, without second thought, claim a letter addressed to you.

You may transpose only one verse tonight, but realize that God can speak as powerfully to your need with a single word as with a whole chapter. That's the wonder of His Spirit moving in your life.

If you do not find a verse that speaks to you tonight or if you do not yet understand transposition, let it be. Another night you can explore the idea again. Try thinking of it as paraphrasing from a personal slant.

Stop now and take stock. If you feel drawn to look for other verses to practice on, God has more instructions to give you.

If you feel weary, and no urgent promptings prevail, your Tutor is dismissing you for this session. As you prepare to go back to bed, pray:

Give me Your peace, Father, for the rest of this night. Whether I sleep or stay awake, I know You will grant me the energy in the morning to face the new day supported by Your Mercy.

Exercise #6 Chasing Away Fear of Sleep (Bible Study/ Directed Meditation)

In chapter 7, some of the reasons people are afraid to go to sleep were discussed. In this exercise you are invited to try Elsie's way of calming herself when she felt beset by strange and frightening forces.[11]

Although you may not be afraid to go to sleep, learning to use your sanctified imagination to invoke a palpable presence of God can be helpful. To have a sanctified imagination means to focus all uses of your imagination on pleasing God.

The first time you try the exercise, be in your special place with your candle lit, your Bible and journal handy. Eventually you will find that your bed is the ideal place for letting God surround you with His protective love, but for now go through the accustomed routine.

Invoke God's protection with the Vaswig Pattern. Reread the episode about Elsie in chapter 7 and record in your journal any points that echo your own situation. If some Bible passage seems relevant note it also, transposing as described in Exercise #5, if you wish. Capture on paper any fragment of thought immediately. These will-o'-the-wisp thoughts often herald new insights which will be given to you as soon as you write down your first vague notion.

Go through the rest of this exercise carefully, so that when you are ready to go back to bed you will remember the directions.

For your second time through the exercise, turn out your light and curl up in a big, comfortable chair, tucking a blanket or comforter around yourself. Essentially, all you need to do is picture God as your Father, who has invited you to sit on His lap because He knows you need comforting and soothing. The chair will be his lap.

As you let yourself relax into the chair, feel how soft yet sturdy it is. Imagine it to be a lap with strong legs under the chair covering, a support and a refuge. If you remember running to be cuddled and soothed by Daddy when you were a child because some fear overtook you, recall that safe, loved, protected feeling now. If you don't have such a childhood memory, let God be the Father you never knew when you were little. . . .

Rest your head against the chair back, snuggle up to it, a small child sheltered from all harm. Imagine you are leaning against God's chest. Let yourself hear the steady beat of His heart. As you listen, notice your own heart calming; with every slowing pulse you hear, "I love you—I am here." God is speaking to you through your own body. . . .

Now turn your attention to the texture of the chair again. Think of it as His robe. Feel the strength of His arms lovingly, easily holding you. As your sanctified imagination takes over, you are no longer afraid. You know He can overcome anything that lurks in the shadows—whether in the room or in your mind. . . .

Gather the blanket or quilt closely around yourself and continue thinking of God's arms around you. Lie back against His arms, letting Him support you totally. Close your eyes if you haven't already.

If fear of things seen or unseen or things you are afraid you will see intrudes, give it to your "Daddy." Paul assures us that as God's adopted daughters and sons we are allowed to use this intimate nickname for God. "Daddy" is our closest equivalent to the biblical *Abba* (Romans 8:15 AMPLIFIED).

You may drift off to sleep while sitting on God's lap, but if you don't, just enjoy being there, His little child, until you feel ready to go back to bed. Once back in bed, you can practice lying back in God's arms to rest and be healed of your fears.

Tomorrow morning, when you get up, remember to thank God for the healing rest you had on His lap, knowing that at any time you choose you can curl up there for comfort again.

Exercise #7 The Secret of the Two Doves (An Imaging Meditation)

> Sleep is like a dove. If you quietly extend your hand, it will light; if you reach for it, it will fly away.[12]

This quote perfectly illustrates the futility of "trying hard," which does *not* get what you want. Any nonsleeper who has wasted many fruitless hours trying to sleep knows this.

Perhaps you find frustration in other areas where you "try hard" to walk the Christ Way. Submission, obedience, "waiting on the Lord" can seem contradictory to that credo, calling for cessation of activity.

As mentioned in chapter 3, "God Has His Reasons," we demand to know why before we obey, as though our approval is needed before we consent—and then we expect instant results.

How strenuously we follow this pattern when we decide we must get back to sleep. We try warm baths, soothing music, long walks in the early evening. We foreswear caffeine drinks, choosing warm milk at bedtime even though we loathe the taste. We try to think only good thoughts. If these fail, we work ourselves to rubber-legged fatigue, put off going to bed until very late, and take sleeping pills—all vain grabs for the dove of sleep. The harder you pursue sleep, the more it flits away.

For the Christian this predicament resembles the current penchant among believers for grabbing at God's Dove, the Holy Spirit. He, too, will elude your clutch. But quietly extend open hands and spirit and He will surround, cover, and empower you with His love, bestowing the gift(s) He chooses for you.

If the preceding six exercises opened any new avenues of worship, contact with God, and any maturing in your outlook on life, then this seventh will help you walk those avenues, set you free to commune with God and "attain . . . the completeness . . . which is nothing less than the standard height of Christ's own perfection . . . the completeness found in Him" (Ephesians 4:13 AMPLIFIED).

This attainment is not to be made during our lifetime, but just the same, we are to point ourselves toward that goal.

★

Imagine, now, a flock of doves whirling up in a flutter of wings like a snowstorm in reverse. As the rushing lift and beat of pinions as they fly about stirs your spirit, you know that only if you stand very still will they softly light again where they had been. In the same way, if you plow into prayer, demanding answers for your insomnia, you could startle the Holy Dove away. Sit quietly, stretching out your hands and your spirit to Him, humbly waiting for His presence, and He will once again drift gently down to surround and shelter you, bringing the tranquil spirit that comes with acceptance. To receive without striving—that is the secret.

This imaging meditation can help you achieve acceptance by putting you into an episode of Jesus' life. Yes, of course it is impossible for you to have lived in His time on earth, but through sanctified imagination you can be present—at Jesus' Baptism.

Although this is a directed meditation, you are free, as always, to choose which actions to take. Who knows, something serendipitous may happen. And what has this to do with insomnia? Come and see. . . .

You are in your accustomed place, you light your candle, you ask God's protection as usual. Now read through the four accounts of Jesus' Baptism in Matthew 3:16, Mark 1:10, Luke 3:22, and John 1:32. Let the different accounts mingle in your mind without making any effort to analyze or compare them. . . . After you have thought about them for as long as you wish, read the following ancient prayer and consider its meanings for you:

> *God be in my head, and in my understanding.*
> *God be in my eyes, and in my looking.*
> *God be in my mouth, and in my speaking.*
> *God be in my heart, and in my thinking.*
> *(God be in my night, and in my waking.*

God be in my sleep, and in my dreaming.)
God be at my end, and at my departing.

Sarum Primer
Fifteenth Century
* *These two lines in parentheses have been added for you.*

Now, sitting still, look at your hands resting upturned in your lap. Let them represent your willingness to receive whatever God wants to give you. Be as open and accepting as you are when you go to the Lord's Table. Close your eyes and compose yourself, using the Tense/Relax method. . . .

Imagine, now, that you are walking down a dusty road in the Holy Land. . . . In the distance, you can see the glitter of a river—it is the Jordan. Many people—men, women, and children—cluster in one spot, and as you draw near, you see they are all watching two men who have waded out into the river. As you wend your way through the crowd no one notices you because they are all so intent on what is happening in the water. . . .

Now you step to the brink of the river; you can hear the water lapping at your feet. Just opposite you, hip-deep in the river, stands one of the men, his back to you. He is very brown and weather-beaten; when he turns his head you see he has wild, shaggy hair and beard, a strongly arched nose, firm, sensitive lips. He is John the Baptist. . . .

The sun sparkles blindingly on the water; the air is full of murmurings from the crowd pressing close. They stand on the banks; some are in the river, watching John. . . .

Standing across from him in the water, His face turned in your direction, is another Man. He is Jesus. His hair, robe, beard, and body are streaming water. He has just been baptized by John. . . .

161

Jesus tips His head back toward heaven, his eyes closed. He holds His arms out slightly, hands palms up. A glorious shimmer of light surrounds Him; perhaps it is more than reflection off the water. . . .

Out of the cloudless sky comes a rumble of thunder; from Luke 3:22 (AMPLIFIED), you know that Jesus is hearing His Father say, "You are My Son, the Beloved! In You I am well pleased and find delight!"

In the air there is a flashing flutter, as of white wings. The Dove of the Holy Spirit is coming down to alight on Jesus as He stands motionless in the water. . . .

Little by little, now, the shimmering light seems to fade. Jesus stirs, opens His eyes, and smiles at John, moving over to hug him warmly. You can hear Jesus thanking His cousin for his obedience in baptizing Him even though John felt unworthy. . . .

Abruptly, you notice that your shoes are wet. You were so wrapped up in what was happening you have stepped into the water. It doesn't matter, though, because just as you discover this, Jesus sees you standing there and wades through the water to your side. . . .

As He comes over to you and you look into His eyes, many thoughts race through your mind. Your feelings about Him become clear, perhaps for the first time. You feel comfortable enough to laugh with Him about your wet shoes, and then to forget them as He reaches out and clasps your hand with His hand, still wet from His Baptism. Whatever your feelings at this moment, let them range. . . .

Standing there by the Jordan with Jesus, you remember what God told John the Baptist: "Upon Whom you shall see the Spirit descend and remain, that One is He Who baptizes with the Holy Spirit" (John 1:33 AMPLIFIED).

Your hand in His, think about this Jesus who loves you, who baptizes with the Holy Spirit. . . . Try to comprehend that He was present with you even before you believed that He is the Son of God. . . .

As you do this, Jesus is watching you with compassion in His eyes; He knows your thoughts. Whatever you want to say to Him at this moment is up to you; He will listen as long as you have something to tell Him. . . .

As soon as you realize you must return to your everyday surroundings, say good-bye to Jesus. As you leave that dusty road and the River Jordan, turn for one last look at Jesus. . . .

Even though you are parting from Him in this experience, you can see, looking into His eyes, a promise that He will be with you still, when you return to the place where you sit in the middle of the night, finding answers about insomnia. . . .

Coming back now, soon you will stir about and open your eyes. Before your impressions fade, record them in your journal. What did you see? How did you feel? Recalling Jesus' attitude of obedience, and John's, think about making them your models for coping with insomnia.

As soon as you are done and have blown out your candle and put things away, one last time picture the moment Jesus waded through the water toward you, His hand outstretched. . . .

References and Suggested Midnight Reading

1. Ronald Enroth, "Sometimes a Fine Line." *Spiritual Counterfeits Projects Newsletter*, July/September 1980, p. 3.

2. David Haddon, "Meditation and the Mind: Mantra vs. the Logos." *Spiritual Counterfeits Newsletter*, January 1982.

3. Ibid.

4. Ibid.

5. Phillip Goldberg and Daniel Kaufman, *Natural Sleep: How to Get Your Share* (Emmaus, Pennsylvania: Rodale Printing, Inc., 1978), pp. 82, 83.

6. Ibid.

7. Ibid.

8. Enroth, "Fine Line," p. 10.

9. Haddon, "Meditation," pp. 1–3.

10. William Vaswig, *At Your Word, Lord* (Minneapolis: Augsburg Publishing House, 1982), pp. 19, 20.

11. See Elsie's story in chapter 7, "God Is Awake, so It's Safe to Sleep."

12. Dietrich Langen, *Speaking of Sleeping Problems*, Medical Advisor Series (New York: Consolidated Book Publishers, 1978), p. 68.

Ten ★

Happiness Will Be—Never to Need Sleep Again

We've arrived at the last questions in our exploration of the meaning of our insomnia: What if all this to-do about sleep were suddenly to become unimportant? Under what circumstances would sleep no longer matter?

Aside from the Parousia—the Second Coming—there is one circumstance only. This way, promised by the Bible and hidden in the phrase "to fall asleep in Jesus," renders sleep forever redundant. I discovered it during my hunt through the Bible for answers to my insomnia when I was more desperate than devout.

The same impulse that moves other just-as-inept believers to say, "There's nothing left to do but pray," finally drove me to the place I, too, should have looked first. Too many of my days were so tangled in the sticky web of unsolved problems I yearned only to crawl into bed and pull forgetfulness over my head. Night after night I lay wide-eyed, dreading the next day's anxiety treadmill. Finally driven to emergency measures, I opened the Bible.

Drawing God's attention to my predicament seemed contradictory because in some vague, unexamined way I was blaming Him for my insomnia. Although at the time I had not admitted it to myself, all I had wanted from God was the warm, fuzzy feeling that He was like a doting grandpa, existing only to make me happy. What a shock to give up this false assumption for the truth. More the schoolmaster, He was determined to teach me how to grow up in Christ. At that point, I began wondering if blaming Him was inaccurate. Rather, was He using my insomnia—or causing it for my good?

I must confess—I still wonder. But at any rate, during that year of intense instruction He made me see that sleep is not indispensable. However much that flies in the face of common opinion, that is true not only for me but for others as well. Risk sleepless nights in the faith that God will give you strength for the next day and you are on your way to the kind of rest that *is* indispensable: resting in the Lord.

This lesson is not easily learned, as I remind myself every time I review the circumstances under which I began learning to trust Him for his Rest. Curiously enough, the insight that resting in Him would eventually restore my ability to sleep came after I had become equally at rest with sleeping or staying awake.

The other truth, which took me years to absorb, is a promise that eventually will make sleep and/or the creative use of sleeplessness irrelevant. By God's definition, only the promised Eternal Life with Christ is Reality, so our single, most valid reason for spending our energies on such conditions of life here as sleep and insomnia is to use them in preparation for entering Reality. How do we do that?

To make us fit to enter Reality, a promise has been given. Here it is: For the born-again, to die is to fall asleep in Jesus. This is the *only* sleep that is death. Because ordinary sleep is *not* death, or any form of it, we need no longer fear the sleep state because we know it is merely another form of consciousness. We also no longer need fear death because Jesus says He will go through it with us into Reality. This is the meaning of falling asleep in Jesus—His arms are open to embrace and protect us at the approach of our death. At that moment, our struggle to sleep becomes forever redundant. Peculiar, isn't it, that the very act of falling asleep, so elusive during life, becomes the solution to our problem?

When we go to be with Christ all our present concerns, including getting to sleep or using wakefulness creatively, will blow away, as useless as dry leaves in the wind. Seemingly important conditions of life such as sleep or insomnia belong to the old order. Our translation into eternal life means we will experience fully the new order brought in by the Alpha and the Omega, who promises He will "make all things new. . . ." What this means we scarcely can comprehend, but we can trust the Infinite One who says it. Resting in His trustworthiness, we believe for the future what we cannot now see.

Once we cease equating sleep with death, the single exception being our last sleep, we can accept the paradox that death is both bondage and freedom. If the Fall had not happened, logic says humankind would have eaten fruit from the Tree of Life with God's permission and become immortal, unhampered by the disobedience of our first parents. But because they flouted God's prohibition and ate the fruit of the Tree of Knowledge, He mercifully prevented His creatures from living forever marred and twisted by sin, by putting them out of the Garden before they could steal eternal life. Intended from the beginning to live forever with God, humankind had to die, instead. But the genius of God, demonstrated in the eviction from the Garden and in the sentence of death He pronounced, was also apparent in His use of death as an instrument of restoration.

In effect, He protected us from ourselves and then, "in the fullness of time," cleared our way home through the perfect death offering of His Surrogate, His Son.

In sharp perception of this primordial God Deed, the ancient martyrs of the Faith, faced with imminent, painful death, realized how blessed they were to be able to "fall asleep in Jesus" in such a way that the rage of their murderers, the pain inflicted by rack and torch and flung stone, simply faded into the distance.

From those martyrs has come one of the greatest prayers of Christendom: "Lord, grant me a blessed death.'" Buoyed by the happy assumption that they could safely die, their prayer trusted God's full provision for their homecoming.

To die blessed—happy—was the privilege of our prototype martyr, Stephen, whose death amid a hail of viciously hurled stones is recorded in heaven as well as in Acts 7:55–60. He died—fell asleep in Jesus—emulating His Lord by interceding for his enemies at the exact moment their rocks battered and tore his flesh.

To impress the importance of being faithful to the last breath, the biblical account slips in another momentous augur for events to come. One cryptic statement in verse 58, "[As] they . . . began to stone him . . . the witnesses placed their garments at the feet of a young man named Saul," identifies one whom God had chosen to be His future champion: Paul. Yes, while Paul was still the relentless persecutor Saul, jailer and murderer of followers of the Christian Way, he was present "and consenting" as a witness to Stephen's death.

Stephen died happy, seeing the heavens opening and the Lord waiting to welcome him home. Ever since, it has been one mark of Christian martyrs to ask God not so much to rescue them from tormentors as to give them strength like Stephen's to die well—to welcome the sleep of death, faithful to their last breath.

We may also contemplate our own death happily, blessed by day-to-day closeness with God, prepared at any moment to meet Him on the other side of death. We can pray to be faithful witnesses, too, living or dying. Then, whether we slip away quietly at a great old age, lose a sudden encounter with a drunk driver, or draw the martyr's lot, we need not fear our final sleep. As someone has well said, "Only when you have come to terms with the fact that you, too, must someday die are you ready to live." For the Christian, that means having your spiritual baggage packed and stacked by the door, ready for imminent departure.

For that reason, nothing is more appropriate, during the silent nocturnal hours, than to work through your own attitude toward living for the Lord, ready for His call at any moment—whether to live or to die. This isn't frightening or morbid if you believe Jesus' promise that to fall asleep in Him means to cross the threshold of Time, when Past, Present, and Future will dissolve into God's Eternal Now. Your slavery to Time shed, and the exigencies of human existence gone, you will move into the

Lord's domain, never again to need relief from pain or worry or sorrow—or insomnia.

What gets in the way of our understanding this, however, is the confusion which has sprung up about sleep and death, to the point where many not only are afraid to think about death but also fear sleep as a sort of dying. A great literary weed patch, of which we are not aware because we have lived so long in the middle of it, chokes our understanding. As shown earlier, sleep is not a "little death" no matter how fondly Homer, Virgil, Shakespeare, and modern poets and writers regard this notion.

Biblically, yes, death is referred to as falling asleep, probably because of certain look-alikes: the supine body, the closed eyes, the familiar personality withdrawn into a remote peace. We have all seen someone so soundly asleep we felt prompted to see if the person was still breathing. That anxiety stems directly from the subtle programming we've absorbed in our reading.

One poet declaims:

> Sleep is a death; O, make me try,
> By sleeping what it is to die,
> And as gently lay my head
> On my grave, as now my bed.[1]

On a similar theme, the eighteenth-century bishop Thomas Ken, who penned the Doxology "Praise God, from whom all blessings flow . . ." took a more relaxed view when he prayed:

> Teach me to live, that I may dread
> The grave as little as my bed.[2]

Both connected death with the bed and sleep. However, it is interesting to speculate on whether the Bishop never had trouble

sleeping or whether he had come to terms with being awake at
night, perhaps using his bonus midnight hours to compose
hymns. With those lines he leaped intuitively into Paul's
assertion, "For me, to live is Christ . . . to die is gain—[the gain
of the glory of eternity].[3]

The Revelation to John makes clear—and the Bishop would
agree—why Paul would yearn to "depart and be with Christ."
John describes the Kingdom of God as a "place" or a "condition"
(no human words suffice to depict it) where the supernal Light
streaming from God's Throne (whatever that means) shines
forever.

Living in the Kingdom, we will no longer partition existence
into "day" and "night." We will no longer experience pain or
sorrow because God will wipe away all reason for tears. Thus, we
can look forward to the last sleep, death, to usher us into the
sublime, the splendorous Omnipresence.

Whether, upon dying, we will sleep all unknowing until the
Christ Triumphant calls us out to put on glory like His, or
whether we will translate in a millisecond after death from this
present consciousness to total consciousness of Him, or whether
the process is something we cannot imagine—it matters not.
Once out of Time's thrall and into God's freedom, Time itself
will become irrelevant. Jesus promises that where He is we will
be, at home in mansions prepared by Him in all His ineffable
hospitality.

We don't have specifics about what we will do when we
awaken in His Kingdom, but we can safely assume He will give
us satisfying work to do. Certainly, we will do more than lie
about on clouds strumming harps. We can also safely assume
that our energy will have no limits, and that there will be joyous

occasions for gathering with others of the community of saints, every eon or so, to report our adventures to Him, maybe coming from the far reaches of the universe to do so. We'll need no rest or sleep or recuperation from our labors because having put on glory like His we will serve Him as tirelessly as the angels who sing, "Holy, Holy, Holy," with never-ending delight and adoration.

Every Christian, woman or man, is entitled to such daydreams.

Speaking of dreams, I recently experienced one that expressed the dearest desire of the insomniac—to be rid of the leaden-legged fatigue that accompanies insomnia when worry takes charge.

Most of us know how impossible it is to run in a dream. The harder you try, the less your legs move. You strain to move as though through molasses.

But in my dream, I was running effortlessly, mile after mile, with a buoyancy so exhilarating my whole body sang. I had no sense of fatigue or breathlessness, my legs ran strong, feet lightly touching the ground. I felt I could run a hundred miles without stopping.

As I ran across a gently rolling countryside, I met others who spoke to me and to whom I spoke, but they seemed to know not to detain me; they knew my purpose was to run. All was joy and serenity, and on I ran. I awoke smiling.

Later, I wondered if this dream was a glimpse of Eternity, where fatigue will be unknown. But then I saw that it was God's way of encouraging me, through my dream, to run my race of life depending on Him to renew my strength. Further, I saw that since being awake sometimes at night is no longer a worry to me, I am to apply the meaning of the dream to other, still troublesome, areas of my life.

Phrases such as "run the good race" and "count it all joy" come to mind from Paul, who again is ready with a "thus saith the Lord."

I remember reading his soliloquy in Philippians 1:21–25, where he speaks of his yearning to depart—"to be free of this world . . ." but where he then decides, ". . . to remain in my body is more needful and essential for your sake. . . . I know that I shall remain and stay by you all, to promote your progress and joy in believing."

What an example he sets us to be couriers, runners with the Good News. Even those who are terminally ill can be such couriers, if they choose to let God see them through to a "blessed death." Their quiet acceptance of impending death cheers and helps every visitor, doctor, nurse, and aide who comes into the room.

My brother, Herbert, as he lay dying of cancer at nineteen, imprinted an image of Christ on my childish heart (I was eleven) with one look that told me, "Jesus is Real." Although he never uttered Jesus' name, his heart spoke to my heart.

His life race had barely begun, yet when he died he'd run his course well; his task was done when he bestowed this mute earnest of God's love upon a little girl who hardly knew the Lord. That look, as though Jesus Himself looked out through my brother's eyes, stayed with me until, at thirty-five, I finally understood the message my brother had given me so long ago.

My dream, my brother—all seem to have come into focus, starting with that first night I couldn't get to sleep, and climaxing when I finally asked God what to do with my wakefulness. . . .

If *you* can't get to sleep, at least consider that He may be speaking to you through your insomnia and that you might miss something wonderful by grabbing for sleep because you dread the aftereffects of a sleepless night. Don't be afraid of discomfort, even though you may be awkward at coping with it. Suffering, in whatever degree, is not fun, and most of us would rather avoid it.

But in Romans 5, Paul suggests a daring idea. He describes the grace given to all who know they are justified through faith, and he invites us to revel in "the hope of the divine splendor that is to be ours." He urges:

> *More than this: let us even exult in our present sufferings, because we know that suffering trains us to endure, and endurance brings proof that we have stood the test, and this proof is the ground of hope. Such a hope is no mockery, because God's love has flooded our inmost heart through the Holy Spirit he has given us.*[4]

Later, after bitter testings and triumphs of his own, Paul reports, "With all our tribulation and in spite of it, I am filled with comfort, I am overflowing with joy."[5]

True, this message of encouragement was intended to stiffen the spines of believers soon to undergo severe tests. The sufferings Paul talked about—the hostility, the unreasoning hatred, cruelty, and rage he and his companions endured for Christ's sake—far outstrip the minor discomforts with which insomniacs deal. But shouldn't there be little trials for baby Christians to cut their milk teeth on? Harder trials come later for those able to chew the tough meat of affliction or persecution.

Or to put it another way, when the novice athlete begins to jump hurdles, the bar is set close to the ground. Only as muscles get stronger and technique improves is the bar raised. Maybe insomnia is a hurdle set close to the ground, to be exchanged for other, higher hurdles as we run our life race.

Beginning as spiritual toddlers, we test our strength as we run, then leap, climb, fall down, scramble over stumbling blocks, claw our way up precipices, swim the torrent. Sometimes we get washed away in the flood and have to crawl out on the bank, where the Lord waits with food and comfort and healing so we can get up and go on with the marathon. Sometimes we wander into the labyrinth or crash into a dead end, but somehow we accept this as part of the way life is. Our spiritual muscles grow stronger.

Or—we sit down and pout, balking at the hurdle we think is too high. So incomprehensible is God's willingness to allow us free choice, He also gives us the right not to attempt the next-highest hurdle. If we refuse His proffered grace, spurn His Spirit of power and love and a sound mind, He allows that, too. Instead, He finds other ways to help us over those hurdles, often without our knowing He has done so. His love is irresistible; He never gives up, even in the face of our rejection.

Because this is true, even the insomniac who refuses to read the Bible on a sleepless night, won't try meditation as a way to peace, feels unfairly condemned to weary nights of not sleeping, won't examine his/her relationship with God, turns a deaf ear to suggestions of making those wakeful hours into bonus times— even for this rebel God will not run out of ideas.

How much better, though, to let in the truth of the observation, ". . . struggles are a gift from God,"[6] and celebrate them with acceptance.

God's Night School Dismissed—for Now

After almost two decades of attending God's night school, I now understand how God used my year of insomnia. My first

175

encounter with sleepless nights, with its tumble of protesting thoughts and emotions, exposed a faith as pretty as cotton candy and just as useless. When daily routines and troubles rushed down upon me like an avalanche, with insomnia the last and heaviest boulder in the slide, my faith *in my faith* lay smashed. I'm convinced that God used this means to tell me to junk this misplaced faith and trust Him instead. He chose to teach me this in the middle of the night.

All thanks go to Him for the habit of daily Bible study and for prayer, however feebly and haltingly it began. I'm grateful for the impulse to write down questions, insights, cries for help and of outrage, captured in a nightly journal. My thoughts took form, then clarified problems not obviously related to my insomnia, and revealed solutions whenever my pen touched paper. God, the perfect Teacher, sat me down like a kept-after-school child, to do my lessons until I got them right. Keep a midnight journal if you want to get in touch with yourself.

When that year of trial and trauma was done and I could look back and see the threshold I'd moved across, by God's grace and guidance, from fear of insomnia to mastery of it, I put my journal away in a drawer as though for a future day. I'm glad I did, because I've often gone back and reviewed what I learned. I've shared those writings with others as I now share them with you. The learning process, like the Hobbit's Road, goes ever on.

Your insomnia experience is different from mine, yet we are comrades. If you have studied the questionnaire and sought your own honest answers; if you have eschewed self-pity, let a little humor lighten the gloom of sleepless nights, and have practiced praising God when you didn't feel like doing so; if you have let silent midnight hours become your bonus times for listening to

God speak from inside you, through His Book and through other people; if the Bible has become your Songbook as you transpose God's music into your own key; if you have brainstormed new ways to use your wakeful nights and are putting them to work; if your being awake in the night has become an invitation to God to teach you whatever He knows you should learn; if the comfort of God's faithfulness daily becomes more real to you; if you take God's prescriptions according to His directions; if you have decided to trust God to stay awake and on guard so you can safely sleep; if you have given the Seven Spiritual Exercises fair trial; and if in your innermost self you have made an appointment to meet the Lord some bright eternal morning and expect to open your eyes from your last sleep to see His smiling face—you are well on your way, by the grace of God, to graduation from His night school. Happy graduation night.

References and Suggested Midnight Reading

1. Sir Thomas Browne, *Religio Medici*, Part II, section 12.

2. Bishop Thomas Ken, "Morning and Evening Hymn."

3. Philippians 1:21 AMPLIFIED.

4. Romans 5:3, 4 NEB.

5. 2 Corinthians 7:4 AMPLIFIED.

6. James McDermott, July 24 entry in *Daily Guideposts 1982* (Carmel, New York: Guideposts Associates, Inc., 1982).

★ ───────────────────────────────

Nine Beatitudes
for Those
Who Lie Awake

ONE   HAPPY are those wakeful ones who meditate on God's goodness rather than moaning, "Poor me," for they shall discover that they are among His beloved.

TWO   HAPPY are those who agree with God in the night watches that they are sinners, for they shall learn how quick He is to forgive.

THREE   HAPPY are the insomniacs who accept God's solutions for their sleeplessness without asking why, for their obedience shall become joy.

FOUR   HAPPY are those whose sleep God disturbs, for He will show them how to use their wakeful hours well.

FIVE   HAPPY are those upon whom God bestows the secret of resting in Him whether asleep or awake, for to them shall be given the gift of intercessory prayer.

SIX   HAPPY are those who rest on God's promises, for His faithfulness gives more refreshing sleep than the best water bed.

SEVEN   HAPPY are those who trust God's prescriptions instead of sleeping pills, for they shall experience only good side effects: Love, Joy, Forbearance, Kindness, Goodness, Faithfulness, Humility, Self-control, and Peace.

EIGHT   HAPPY are those who believe it is safe to sleep, for they shall know that God keeps watch over them night and day.

NINE   HAPPY are those whom God calls to their final sleep in Jesus, for they shall awaken at last to look into His Face.